KASHMIR
THE ECONOMICS OF PEACE BUILDING

A Report of the CSIS South Asia Program
with the Kashmir Study Group

Author
Teresita C. Schaffer

2005

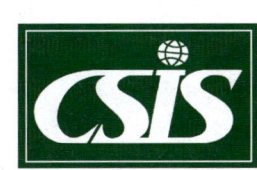

About CSIS

The Center for Strategic and International Studies (CSIS) provides strategic insights and practical policy solutions to decisionmakers committed to advancing global security and prosperity. Founded in 1962 by David M. Abshire and Admiral Arleigh Burke, CSIS is a bipartisan, nonprofit organization headquartered in Washington, D.C., with more than 220 employees. Former U.S. senator Sam Nunn became chairman of the CSIS Board of Trustees in 1999, and John J. Hamre has led CSIS as its president and chief executive officer since 2000.

CSIS experts, working through more than 25 programs, conduct research and analysis and develop policy initiatives grouped under three themes:

Defense and Security Policy. Currently devoting over a third of its resources to security issues, CSIS has chosen to focus both on the traditional drivers of national security—defense policy and organization—and some of the most important new dimensions of international security, such as post-conflict reconstruction, proliferation, and homeland security.

Global Trends. A growing and more mobile population and advances in economics and technology have exposed the inability of nationally organized governments to respond to transnational challenges. A large number of international organizations, multinational corporations, and nongovernmental entities now exert significant influence over international affairs. CSIS examines not only how traditional nation-states themselves deal with problems that cross national boundaries, but also how they relate to this new and powerful group of actors.

Regions. CSIS is the only institution of its kind with resident programs on all the world's major regions. The programs enable CSIS to anticipate developments in key countries and regions across the world, especially as they affect global security.

CSIS does not take specific policy positions; accordingly, all views expressed herein should be understood to be solely those of the author(s).

Photo Credit
Climber and Sherpas on Nun Kun
© Galen Rowell/CORBIS

Library of Congress Cataloging-in-Publication Data
CIP information available upon request
ISBN 0-89206-480-3

.

The CSIS Press
Center for Strategic and International Studies
1800 K Street, N.W., Washington, D.C. 20006
Tel: (202) 775-3119
Fax: (202) 775-3199
E-mail: books@csis.org
Web: www.csis.org/

Contents

List of Illustrations

Preface and Acknowledgments

The inspiration for this report, and the resources that made it possible, came from Farooq Kathwari. A dedicated son of Kashmir and a passionate believer in the American dream, Farooq asked CSIS, together with the Kashmir Study Group that he had founded in 1997, to take a hard and creative look at the economic side of peacemaking in Kashmir. Without his vision and support we could not have carried out this project; without his ideas, it would have been much poorer. He has had my friendship for 20 years. He has my profound thanks as well.

We also benefited from the help and input of many people in India, Pakistan, Kashmir, and the United States. During my all too brief visit to Jammu and Kashmir (J&K), senior members of the state government were kind enough to make time for me. I enjoyed the gracious hospitality of Amitabh Mattoo, vice chancellor of Jammu University and of the Srinagar Chamber of Commerce, and learned an enormous amount from my conversations in both Jammu and Srinagar. Special thanks to M.Y. Khan, at that time chairman of the Jammu and Kashmir Bank, who not only interrupted his travel schedule to spend time briefing me on the financial picture in J&K but shared his insights by giving a memorable talk at CSIS. Wajahat Habibullah, a member of the Kashmir Cadre of the Indian Administrative Service who served in several senior positions in the state, gave generously of his advice and insights about how the state government and economy work. I am grateful for the suggestions I received from academic and business figures such as Gulam Rusull Khan in Srinagar, Suba Chandran at the Institute for Peace and Conflict Studies in Delhi, Faisal Bari at the Lahore University of Management Sciences, Rizwan Zeb at the Institute for Strategic Studies in Islamabad, and Shahid Javed Burki of the Emerging Markets Partnership. Government officials in Srinagar, Jammu, Delhi, Muzaffarabad, and Islamabad took time to see me and share their thoughts. U.S.-based Kashmiris were likewise generous with their time and ideas.

My colleagues in the Kashmir Study Group listened patiently to an early draft of this report and provided invaluable feedback. Joseph Schwartzberg went through several drafts, which were much improved by his careful attention. Philip Schwartzberg prepared the maps in this study.

My small office at CSIS has assembled a remarkable number of talented and dedicated people whose contribution to the project was tremendous. Mandavi Mehta, who had just completed two years as my right hand and research associate, spent a week in J&K and helped me find some key sources of basic economic information. Pramit Mitra, her successor and my close colleague at CSIS, has kept the program humming. And among the interns who have volunteered in our program, I am especially grateful to Bidisha Biswas, Santosh Sagar, Bushra Asif, Maha Qazi, Bethany Tindall, Joseph Puthenveetil, and Divyesh Lalloobhai.

Whatever insights this report is able to provide owe a great deal to all these people—and to the many others with whom we spoke in the course of this project. The errors that remain are mine alone.

Introduction and Executive Summary

The Kashmir problem is the most intractable part of the dispute between India and Pakistan. In the past five decades, scholars and statesmen have analyzed the political dimensions of the problem many times over and have tried to solve it or at least to manage it. The economic dimensions of the problem have received much less attention.

Kashmir today is reeling under the impact of an earthquake measuring 7.6 on the Richter scale, with its epicenter between the capital of the Pakistani side of Kashmir and the Line of Control (LOC). It has left some 70,000 dead, even more wounded, and an estimated 3 million homeless facing the Himalayan winter. This report does not attempt to make a detailed assessment of the relief and reconstruction needs of the region; others are better equipped for that task. We have, however, reflected in this report some of the most urgent requirements for rebuilding infrastructure and some of the key opportunities for bringing Kashmiris from both sides of the line together in a rebuilding effort.

The lesson of the first anxious days following the earthquake is clear, however. This is a time for decisive action and a bold vision for a better future in Kashmir. We urge those who are frustrated with over half a century of stalemate in Kashmir to think big, both about new ways of responding to a tragedy and, more importantly, about finding a new and more cooperative model for bringing both economic life and political hope to a region that has had too little of either. The report's recommendations should be read in that spirit.

This study is an effort to address the lack of economic content in thinking on Kashmir. Starting from an assessment of the current economic picture in Kashmir, both the parts administered by India and those administered by Pakistan, it will attempt to define how economics might help to build peace. It will look at two levels:

- In the near term, measures that could be taken in the absence of major political change to build up peace constituencies and lay the groundwork for a peaceful future; and

- In the longer term, measures that could reinforce a long-term settlement and leave a more prosperous Kashmir integrated with the regional and world economies.

The study presents a long list of recommendations, a kind of cafeteria from which policymakers can draw, some capable of implementation by one side acting alone, others requiring joint action. All, however, could be implemented under a variety of political arrangements. They draw on Kashmir's natural resources and its skillful, entrepreneurial population, and they attempt to steer clear of the problems created by long-term violence. Some initiatives would also require the participation of nongovernmental organizations and civil society. None should be read as a hidden appeal for any particular design of a settlement.

Economic interventions are not a substitute for fundamental political decisions or for the long and complex process of changing political behavior. Our hope in presenting this report is that policymakers will find in it economic tools that can facilitate the political changes that people in the region so badly need.

The Kashmiri Economies

Kashmir includes five different regions. Since the end of the war that followed the independence of India and Pakistan, three parts of the former princely state of Jammu and Kashmir have been under Indian administration: the Kashmir region itself (including the Valley of Kashmir), with a predominantly Muslim population, regarded by all parties as the heart of both the region and the problem; Jammu, south of Kashmir, with a Hindu majority; and Ladakh, a sparsely populated high mountain plateau area east of Kashmir proper. Two have been administered by Pakistan: Azad Kashmir, a thin strip between Kashmir proper and the Pakistani province of Punjab; and the Northern Areas, another mountainous and sparsely settled area. Both are entirely Muslim. This report does not deal with the parts of Kashmir that are administered by China. We have used the shorthand "J&K" to refer to the Indian parts of Kashmir, "AJK" to refer to Azad Kashmir, and "NA" to refer to the Northern Areas.

Sluggish production of major agricultural crops, a devastating lack of jobs, especially outside the government, and a poor investment climate are among the serious problems shared across the Line of Control. Though some sectors have done well—horticulture and handicrafts in J&K, and construction and the security "industry" on both sides of the line—dependence on government transfers is extraordinarily high. On both sides, the state government is the largest nonagricultural employer.

Jammu and Kashmir

On the Indian side of the line, J&K's sluggish growth and a decade of stagnation in per capita income coexist with a relatively high level of per capita consumption. The percentage of people in poverty is no higher than in the rest of India and may be lower. Literacy is significantly lower than for India as a whole, but spending on education and health is well above the national average.

Infrastructure is a problem area. J&K has tremendous unrealized potential for hydroelectric power, and electrical generators lose nearly half their output to transmission and distribution losses. Rail lines stop at Jammu; road links both within Kashmir and to the rest of India are inadequate and now badly disrupted by the earthquake. Telecommunications have improved significantly in the past five years, but teledensity is still only half the level of the rest of India. Air travel is especially important given the problems of land transport.

Environmental degradation has taken an alarming toll. Water pollution will have lasting health effects and will undermine both agriculture and efforts to revive tourism. Kashmir's forests, which should be a major resource, are being depleted by illegal logging.

Looking sector by sector at the economy, major agricultural crops have stagnated in the past decade, but horticulture has done well, in some ways benefiting from changes in marketing patterns induced by the insurgency. Tourism all but disappeared during the worst years of the insurgency but has recovered to about one-third of its pre-1989 level. Economic and industrial revival programs from both the state and the national governments have moved slowly and have had limited effects. Until the security situation improves, major changes in the investment picture are unlikely.

These problems affect all parts of J&K. Jammu is less affected than the Valley of Kashmir by insecurity; hence, it has done slightly better in attracting investment. Jammu also supports a significant population of Hindus driven out of the Valley of Kashmir by the insurgency. Everyone agrees that the Pandits, as they are called, must be reintegrated, but no preparations for that kind of integration have been made. Ladakh has two additional problems: physically, it is most easily accessible through Kashmir and consequently affected by the insecurity there; and its harsh but fragile environment is under tremendous pressure.

Azad Kashmir and the Northern Areas

The two areas administered by Pakistan are quite distinct, physically and in every other way. Azad Kashmir has per capita income substantially below that of the rest of Pakistan. Literacy, however, is substantially above the rest of Pakistan, and the situation of women compares favorably with the national scene. Its economy is driven chiefly by agriculture but also relies heavily on remittances. The southern part of Azad Kashmir sends many young men to the Pakistan army; others go to Europe or the Persian Gulf. Tourism has some potential but is essentially undeveloped. The state government, with national support, is supporting a refugee population of some 54,000, many of whom have come to Azad Kashmir from Indian-administered parts of the state. Individual refugees have little incentive to become self-supporting, because they lose financial benefits if they leave the refugee support system. Azad Kashmir is home to most of those killed or wounded by the earthquake and to many of the homeless. Relief and reconstruction will be its major preoccupation for the next year or so.

The Northern Areas have an income level just over half that of the rest of Pakistan, low health and literacy, and a high incidence of poverty. However, they have made remarkable progress on the social side in the past 20 years, thanks in part to remarkable work by the Aga Khan Rural Support Program. This region is sparsely populated and remote and will always be somewhat of a "niche" pastoral economy, but it has begun to develop an interesting tourism industry following the opening of the Karakorum Highway.

Recommendations

The recommendations in this report aim at improving the economy and increasing the linkages between the regions of Kashmir and between Kashmir and the surrounding countries. Ultimately, this will require a more vigorous private economy. Private investment in J&K is unlikely to pick up until security conditions have improved, however. In AJK and the Northern Areas, the absence of a settlement and their relative remoteness from Pakistan's economic heartland discourage investment.

Our recommendations are organized into 11 topical clusters. Many can be carried out unilaterally, without coordination between India and Pakistan. These include economic development initiatives, employment programs, much of the needed infrastructure creation, and environmental cleanup. The most powerful of these unilateral measures include:

■ *Expanding employment* on both sides, using badly needed public works in such areas as road building and environmental cleanup.

■ *Creating in Srinagar the business services needed to expand trade, including a one-stop "dry port"* that provides export documentation, packaging, and customs processing; bonded trucking and rail service; and a container depot featuring containers small enough to fit through the road tunnels leading into and out of J&K. This would be the lead item in an overall program intended to expand trade between Kashmir and both India and Pakistan, as well as with the outside world.

■ *Designating Srinagar Airport as an international airport with the full range of services*, so as to permit direct exports, charter flights for tourists, and eventually package tourist deals including destinations on both sides of the Line of Control.

■ *Developing refugee resettlement plans* for both the Hindu Pandits driven out of the Valley of Kashmir and the refugees in AJK. Both groups are suffering, and risk becoming obstacles to a settlement unless they are given a stake in peace.

■ *Encouraging India to open up J&K to foreign bilateral aid donors.* Current Indian policy limiting the foreign aid presence to multilateral donors cuts off an important avenue of funding for development projects in J&K. Bilateral aid could play an important role in financing many of the initiatives put forth in this report.

The most powerful engines of economic growth and integration require joint action and, in several cases, private support. Some of these are practicable today and could be looked on as early steps in a peace process that is likely to last at least several years. Others should be considered as ingredients in an eventual settlement. The key recommendations in this category are:

■ *Integrating earthquake relief and reconstruction activities across the Line of Control,* and developing integrated plans for future disasters.

■ *Opening the road between the two sides of Kashmir to trade and truck traffic,* which both Indians and Pakistanis are in principle willing to do. The initiation of bus service has whetted people's appetites for more.

■ *Joint initiatives on water management and the environment,* under which local authorities in AJK and J&K meet periodically, exchange data on water quality and water flows, and consult with one another on environmental problems they share. Pakistan's and AJK's rivers all flow through J&K first, and water quality as well as water supply are an increasingly urgent issue in the region.

■ *A Joint Kashmir Tourism Development Board,* composed primarily of representatives of the tourist-related industries in AJK, the Northern Areas, and J&K, but also including representatives of the AJK and J&K governments and observers from Islamabad and New Delhi. It would facilitate the development of facilities and commercial packages bringing tourists to both sides of Kashmir.

■ *Linking the electricity grids on both sides of Kashmir.* Hydroelectric power is one of the most important resources in AJK and an important potential resource in J&K. The two sides' needs are complementary, and a grid connection would sidestep the restrictions on power development in Kashmir under the Indus Waters Treaty. It is not too early to start looking at concrete ways of managing the political risk this would involve.

■ *An ecological science park near the Siachen and Baltoro Glaciers.* A proposal for such a park has been under development for some time, and studies by scientists affirm its likely scientific value. It would serve as a powerful symbol of a new India-Pakistan relationship. The current cease-fire along the Line of Control makes it possible to think seriously about such a proposal. It would have to be preceded by an understanding between the Indian and Pakistani armies on demilitarizing the Siachen area.

The recommendations listed above, as well as the others contained in the main body of this report, would all contribute to our twin goals of economic improvement and peace-building, but they are inherently limited. Our final recommendation is more ambitious and more visionary. It would open up the possibility of a more dynamic and prosperous economy extending not only to Kashmir but throughout the region.

■ *Creating a special economic zone in all of Kashmir, with duty-free access to India and Pakistan and including an institutional framework for joint investment.* This would build on the trade liberalization agreements reached within the South Asian Association for Regional Cooperation (SAARC). Taking as a point of departure the framework that now exists in both India and Pakistan for export promotion zones, it would provide not only for duty-free exports to India and Pakistan, but also for duty-free imports of inputs, for appropriate tax breaks and especially regulatory simplification for participating enterprises, and for accelerated creation of the necessary infrastructure. It would place considerable demands on the governance structure on both sides, to ensure that the tax and import duty treatment did not lead to abuses. The tourism, transportation, electric power, and information technology sectors would be promising areas for investment.

Such an arrangement could be implemented under a variety of political and territorial settlements of Kashmir. It would be a departure from current economic policies in India and Pakistan and from the patterns prevalent in India-Pakistan relations. But both India and Pakistan have taken significant steps in the past 10 years to integrate their economies with the rest of the world and with their neighbors in South Asia. In that sense, a "Kashmir Special Economic Zone" represents a logical extension of the policies both countries have been trying to implement.

All the recommendations for joint action require more India-Pakistan cooperation than is in practice today. The proposal for a special economic zone requires major changes in the domestic economic policies of both countries and, indeed, a new way of looking at economic relationships. Even some of the unilateral recommendations require rethinking the relationship between both parts of Kashmir and the ties between India and Pakistan, as well as the parts of Kashmir they currently hold. This will take time.

This is not a reason to set them aside, however. Rather, it is an argument for creating a more peaceful environment in which they can succeed. As part of that process, we have included a series of recommendations for academic and cultural exchanges. These may not, strictly speaking, be economic proposals, but they would, if implemented, help lay the groundwork for this more ambitious vision of what Indians, Pakistanis, and Kashmiris might accomplish together.

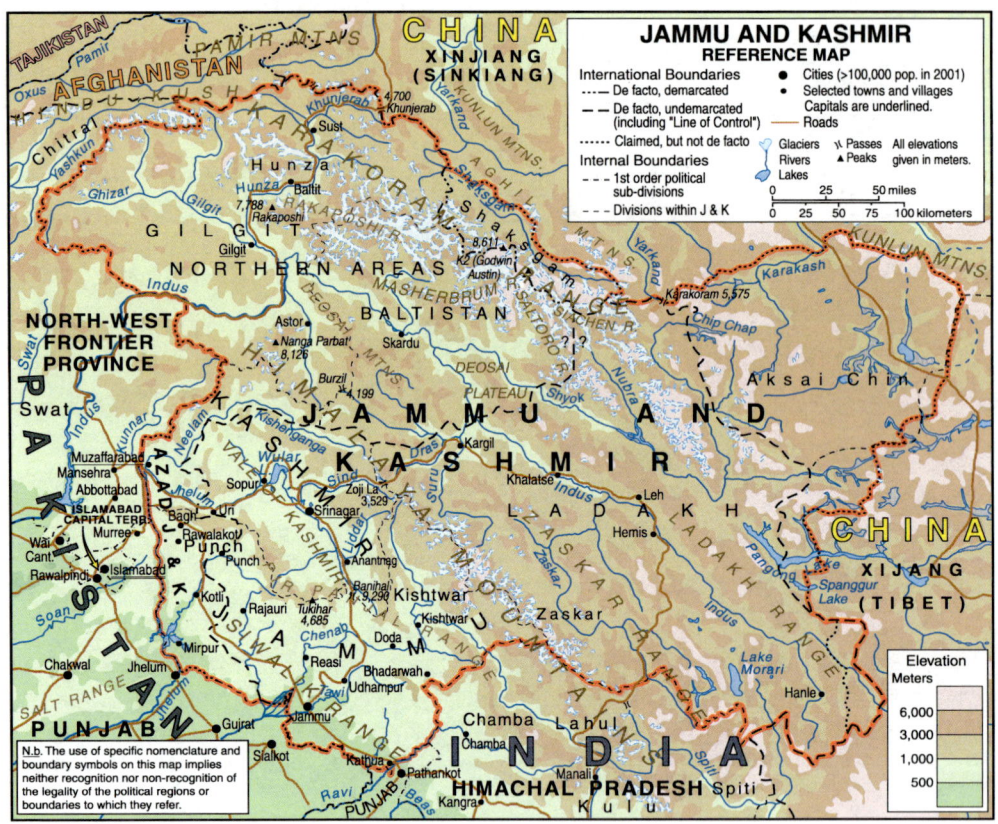

What Is Kashmir?

The former princely state of Jammu and Kashmir is a physically and culturally diverse area, consisting of 13.86 million people spread out across 187,180 square kilometers.[1] The state is divided administratively into five regions, three controlled by India and two by Pakistan. They are separated by a line, known as the Line of Control (LOC), that has remained substantially the same since the Indian and Pakistani armies concluded the first of their Kashmir-based wars in 1949.

There are, in addition, two parts of the old princely state that are administered by China: the Aksai Chin region, and those areas that Pakistan ceded to China in its 1963 border agreement. India considers these areas part of the princely state and hence claims them; neither Pakistan nor China accepts this claim. This report will not deal with the Chinese-administered parts of the old princely state.

For brevity's sake, in this study we will refer to the parts of Kashmir administered by India as Jammu and Kashmir (J&K) and to those administered by Pakistan as Azad Jammu and Kashmir (AJK) and the Northern Areas (NA). "Kashmiris" refers to residents of any part of the old princely state, and "ethnic Kashmiris" refers to those whose cultural and linguistic heritage is bound up with the Kashmiri language.

Each of these five regions has a distinct culture, with its own mix of the many languages spoken and different religions practiced within the region. The part that both India and Pakistan consider to be the heart of the state is the province of Kashmir, including especially the densely populated Valley of Kashmir. It is overwhelmingly Muslim, Kashmiri speaking, with perhaps the most complex economy and the strongest political significance for Kashmiris, Indians, and Pakistanis. But both politically and economically, the diversity of the state presents a special challenge: just as Kashmiris, especially on the Indian side of the LOC, chafe at being dominated by the national authorities in Islamabad and New Delhi, the people of regions of the state outside the Valley of Kashmir do not wish to be dominated by the Muslims of the valley, nor are their economic interests always congruent with those of the valley.

Regions Administered by India: Jammu and Kashmir

Valley of Kashmir

The heart of J&K is the vale, or Valley of Kashmir, on the upper Jhelum River. The capital of J&K, Srinagar, is located within the valley, astride the Jhelum. The soil is

---

1. Area does not include disputed territory claimed by China.

well watered and fertile and supports intensive agriculture. The natural beauty of the region is a draw for tourists in ordinary times. Kashmir is the most densely populated region with 5.4 million people living on 15,948 square kilometers of land. The population of the valley today is close to 100 percent Muslim and overwhelmingly Sunni. Most of the significant and prominent Hindu minority, known as Pandits, left or were forced out during the insurgency in the 1990s. Though the Kashmiri language is spoken by more people than any other in the state, it is confined primarily to the province of Kashmir, where roughly 90 percent of the population speaks Kashmiri. Approximately 8 percent of the province's people, mainly in the mountains surrounding the vale, speak one of the many local languages, such as Gojri, or dialects, known collectively as Pahari. These languages have been lumped together under the term "Hindi" by the 2001 Indian Census, and it is not possible to disaggregate them.

Jammu

Separated from the Valley of Kashmir by the Pir Panjal mountain range, Jammu is the second most-populous region in J&K. Its terrain is primarily hilly, the valleys are farmed, and there is a narrow strip of land that can support intensive agriculture. The areas that have not been cleared for cultivation support dense forests. Jammu has 4.4 million people living in an area of 26,000 square kilometers. Approximately two-thirds of the people are Hindu, while less than 30 percent are Muslims. Two districts of Jammu have Muslim majorities. Additionally, there are a significant number of Sikhs in both Jammu and Kashmir. The dominant language in Jammu is Dogri, a Punjabi language spoken by 53 percent of the population. Nearly 30 percent of the population speaks one of the languages classified as Hindi by the 2001 census.

Ladakh

Ladakh is physically the largest region within Indian-held Kashmir, comprising nearly half the area of the state. Its topography, including some of the world's highest mountains and a high plateau, and its arid climate make life extremely difficult. Ladakh can only support small-scale agriculture along with sheep, goat, and yak herding. It is sparsely populated, with only 233,000 people in an area of 59,000 square kilometers. Over half the people are Buddhists, with Muslims running a close second at 46 percent. Unlike in J&K, Muslims in Ladakh, particularly around Kargil, are mainly Shia. The overwhelming majority of Ladakhis, over 90 percent, speaks Tibetan dialects.[2]

J&K is governed like other states in India, with an elected legislative assembly and a state government formed by the majority in the assembly and headed by a chief minister. The governor is appointed by the central government in Delhi, although in certain circumstances, the Indian constitution provides for the governor to rule directly, superseding the government. The constitution includes special

---

2. All population figures are from Office of the Registrar General, "Tables Showing Provisional Census Results—State & District Level," Census of India 2001, http://www.censusindia.net/cendata1/, accessed August 18, 2005.

authorities for J&K not available to other states (Article 370): as originally written, the central government in Delhi was to be responsible only for foreign affairs, defense, and communications. Over the years, Delhi's jurisdiction has expanded, but J&K still retains some unique rights. Most importantly, these include land ownership, which is restricted to residents of the state. Administratively, J&K is divided into three regions, corresponding to the regions described above. The Kashmir region includes six districts; the Jammu region, six; and the Ladakh region, two.

Regions Administered by Pakistan: Azad Jammu and Kashmir and the Northern Areas

Azad Jammu and Kashmir

Pakistani-controlled AJK has very similar terrain to Jammu. Its estimated 3 million people are situated on 13,297 square kilometers of land. The population is almost entirely Muslim, with a clear Sunni majority.[3] Over 80 percent of the population speaks Punjabi. Its government is headed by a president and a state council of 12 members, supported by a locally elected legislature. AJK is also represented in the Pakistani parliament. In practice, the Pakistan Ministry of Kashmir Affairs plays a substantial, even dominant, role in the local government.

Northern Areas

The Pakistani-controlled Northern Areas are by far the largest region within Kashmir. At nearly 72,496 square kilometers in area, this region is larger than all of Indian-administered Kashmir.[4] It is an arid, mountainous region and supports only a small, pastoral economy. The Northern Areas contain the greater part of the Karakoram Mountains, which include K2 and are a favored destination of mountaineers. The NA have a total population of 870,000, virtually all of whom are Muslims; the majority, however, are Shia. The two dominant languages are Shina and Balti. The NA are administered separately from AJK and are ruled directly from Islamabad through the Northern Areas Council, headed by Pakistan's minister for Kashmir affairs. The area comprises five districts. Residents of the NA do not elect members to the Pakistan National Assembly and are not taxed, but they do benefit from a number of special subsidies.

Note on the Earthquake of October 8, 2005

On October 8, 2005, an earthquake measuring 7.6 on the Richter scale struck the region, with its epicenter between Muzaffarabad, the capital of AJK, and the Line of

---

3. Government of Azad Jammu & Kashmir, http://www.ajk.gov.pk/site/index.php?option=com_content &task=view&id=2257&Itemid=144, accessed August 18, 2005.

4. Usman Ali Iftikhar, "Population, Poverty and Environment: Northern Areas Strategy for Sustainable Development," background paper, International Union for the Conservation of Nature and Natural Resources (IUCN), Karachi, 2003.

Control. Its most severe impact was in AJK and in Pakistan. Estimated earthquake-related deaths as this report went to press exceeded 70,000, with the number of injured over 74,000. In the town of Muzaffarabad, an estimated 80 percent of the buildings were destroyed, including the elaborate government complex on the outskirts of the town. The earthquake struck close to 9:00 a.m., so when school buildings collapsed, they fell on full classrooms, resulting in a tremendous number of children killed or hurt. Whole families, and in some cases whole villages, were wiped out. An estimated 3 million people are without their normal shelter. Much of the affected area is in the foothills of the Himalayas. Under the best of circumstances, access was bound to be difficult; in some areas helicopters were the only viable way of reaching affected areas. With winter upon them, provision of shelter from the elements is a life-and-death issue for many of the newly homeless.

On the Indian side, the areas most severely affected were small communities close to the Line of Control. The death toll was reported at close to 1,500 as of early December 2005, with an estimated 6,600 injured. Here too, 100,000 people were left homeless. Some 32,000 to 40,000 houses were damaged, and half the official buildings were leveled. Some villages lost virtually their entire housing stock. Cold weather will add to the casualties. Media attention and relief work have been most intense in the area near the Srinagar-Muzaffarabad road; in other areas, there are complaints that desperately needed aid or supplies have not arrived.[5] An estimated 35,000 tents are needed to provide temporary shelter; less than half were in place a week after the disaster. Electricity and kerosene are scarce. Many residents have to rely on kangris, the traditional Kashmiri heater carried underneath a woolen outer garment.[6] Rebuilding work has begun, but it will be a race against time. As of October 25, press reports indicated that 130 homes, schools, and other structures had been rebuilt.[7] There is some concern about improving the structural integrity of any new structures that go up in the region.

The earthquake also disrupted land transportation throughout the region, including the road from Srinagar to Muzaffarabad, across the Line of Control, which was recently opened to bus travel, and the road from Srinagar to Delhi. Both to provide access for relief workers and to preserve the bus route, restoration of the roads is taking a high priority.

India and Pakistan have responded in accordance with their quite different traditional approaches to disaster relief. In India, the relief effort has been carried out by the national and state governments, with substantial help from the army. Local and Indian nongovernmental relief organizations have also been active, and some of them have received support from abroad. In recent disasters, India has not accepted foreign assistance for relief but has accepted it for reconstruction.

In Pakistan, the central government, and specifically the army, have been at the center of the relief effort. They have requested and received substantial assistance

---

5. Aijaz Hussain, "Kashmir Quake: India's Disaster—Deadly Delay," *India Today*, October 17, 2005.

6. Agence France-Presse, "Indian Kashmir Quake Survivors Appeal for Traditional Heaters," October 21, 2005.

7. Syed Basharat, "In Devastated Uri, People Try to Start Life Again," *Kashmir Times*, October 25, 2005.

from overseas, including military helicopter rescue teams from the United States and support from a variety of national and multinational organizations and non-governmental organizations (NGOs) already active in Pakistan. Other donors include UNICEF, the Aga Khan Foundation, and the Red Cross and Red Crescent Societies.

Efforts to mobilize international funds are still under way. The World Bank announced a $470-million reconstruction package for Pakistan on October 25. The UN has appealed for $550 million in additional funding. A UN-led meeting in Geneva the week of October 25 pushed for early disbursement of the pledges already recorded.

India offered assistance to the harder-hit Pakistan soon after the quake. Pakistan accepted that help, with some restrictions especially involving India's offer of helicopters. India was reported to have shipped 25 tons of supplies to Pakistan. India and Pakistan have established modalities and five access points for quake-affected Kashmiris to cross the Line of Control for relief purposes. There are the inevitable complaints about relief operations, but there are also stories about cooperation across the LOC, some of it involving Indian and Pakistani military personnel. Telephone communications across the LOC have been eased. Not surprisingly, each of these moves is fraught with emotion and the underlying situation is full of frustrations.

It is still too early to assess the longer-term impact of this disaster on the region. It will not change the fundamental structure of the economy on either side of the LOC, though it will leave a legacy of rebuilding requirements that runs the risk of pushing longer-term economic priorities to the side.

Demographic and Economic Profile by Region

	Jammu	Kashmir	Ladakh	J&K Total	India	Azad Kashmir	Northern Areas	AJK Total	Pakistan
Area (sq. km.)	26,293	15,948	59,146	101,387	2,973,190	13,297	72,496	85,793	778,720
Population (in millions)	4.395 (2001)	5.441 (2001)	0.232 (2001)	10.070 (2001)	1,080.26 (2005 est.)	2.916 (1998)	0.870 (1998)	3.786 (1998)	162.420 (2005 est.)
Population density (persons/sq. km.)	167	341	4	99	363	219	12	44	209
Life expectancy at birth	[n.a.]	[n.a.]	[n.a.]	59.4, males; 64.2, females (1992)	63.57, males; 65.16, females (2005 est.)	56, males; 55, females (1998)	56.5 (2001)	[n.a.]	61 (2001)
Infant mortality rate (per 1,000 live births)	[n.a.]	[n.a.]	[n.a.]	64 (1994–1998)	56.29 (2005 est.)	95 (1988)	70 (2001)	[n.a.]	81.5 (2001)
Percent literate	62.79 (2001)	47.33 (2001)	60.25 (2001)	54.46 (2001)	65 (2001)	61 (1998)	33 (1998)	55 (1998)	45.7 (2005 est.)
Income per capita	[n.a.]	[n.a.]	[n.a.]	$280 (2001–2002 est.)	$472 (2001)	$184 (1998)	$164 (1998)	$179 (1998)	$446 (2001)
Percent urban	22.81 (2001)	26.92 (2001)	16.09 (2001)	24.88 (2001)	27.8 (2001)	12	14	12	32.5 (1998)

Sources:

India info

Percentage Urban, Literacy: 2001 Census

http://www.censusindia.net/cendata1/show_data54.php3?j=100&j1=1&j2=1&j3=Jammu+&+Kashmir

Income Per Capita: Economist Intelligence Unit Pakistan Afghanistan Country Profile 2001, p. 21

All other data from CIA World Factbook

http://www.cia.gov/cia/publications/factbook/index.html

Pakistan info:

Percentage Urban: 1998 Census

http://www.statpak.gov.pk/depts/pco/statistics/area_pop/area_pop.html

Life expectancy and Infant Mortality: Iftikhar, Population, Poverty and Environment, p. 16

http://www.northernareas.org.pk/nassd/background_papers.htm

Income Per Capita: Economist Intelligence Unit Pakistan Afghanistan Country Profile 2001, p. 21

All other data from CIA World Factbook

http://www.cia.gov/cia/publications/factbook/index.html

J and K info:

Population: 2001 census

Percentage Urban: calculated from 2001 Census cited in Indian Planning Commission (IPC), p.28

Literacy: 2001 census cited in IPC report, p. 26

Infant Mortality: National Family Health Survey II. The Planning Commission's Jammu and Kashmir Development Report shows a state infant mortality rate of 45, based on the Sample Registration System, but notes that its figures are "not reliable" because of collection problems due to the insurgency.
http://www.nfhsindia.org/pnfhs2.html

Life Expectancy: Sample Registration System of India cited in Health Administrator Journal of the Indian Society of Health Administrators, July 2004 Vol XVI, http://medind.nic.in/haa/t04/i1/haat04i1c.shtml

http://medind.nic.in/haa/t04/i1/haat04i1p46.pdf

Income per Capita: Dollar figures are computed using the exchange rates for the year in question, from the Ministry of Finance web site

Jammu, Kashmir, and Ladakh info:

Population, Literacy, and Percentage Urban: 2001 India Census

Azad Kashmir info:

All information from 1998 census cited in International Bank for Development and Reconstruction 2001 Social Assessment Report, Development Consortium - (wbreport1.pdf)

Northern Areas:

Area: Iftikhar, p.9

http://www.northernareas.org.pk/nassd/background_papers.htm

Population, Percentage Urban, Literacy: 1998 census cited in Iftikhar

Infant Mortality, Life Expectancy: Northern Areas Health Project Baseline Survey (2002) cited in Iftikhar

Per Capita Income: Iftikhar, p. 11 (the figure given is PKR 7500, converted at the exchange rate for the year in question of PKR 46 per $1)

AJK Total info:

Information calculated using data from Azad Kashmir and Northern Areas data

The Indian Side: An Economic Snapshot of Jammu and Kashmir

Jammu and Kashmir presents a mosaic of contrasts and paradoxes. Kashmiris speak of the past decade and a half as an unmitigated disaster for the economy and for people's lives, but a look at the figures suggests that there are both great weaknesses and some surprising high points in the economic record of J&K during that period. It combines low growth performance with relatively low measured poverty rates, weak investment with a vigorous entrepreneurial tradition, sluggish production of major crops with tremendous potential in horticulture, crumbling infrastructure with unusually high dependence on government funds.

Population, Urbanization, Health, and Education

The population of Jammu and Kashmir grew by 29 percent between 1991 and 2001, for an annual rate of 2.55 percent, compared with a national rate of 1.9 percent.[1] Just under 25 percent of the population is urban, slightly lower than the national figure of 28 percent. Within the urban areas, the fastest growth took place in the two largest urban areas, which expanded by 60 percent between 1981 and 2001. Only two districts, Srinagar and Jammu, are heavily urbanized.[2]

The 2001 Indian census figures show 900 females for every 1,000 males in J&K, compared with a national average of 933 and levels above 1,000 in most countries in the world. The sex ratio is sometimes considered a rough measure of the health of a population and its treatment of women.[3] In general, the ratio of women to men is lower in the cities, reflecting in-migration of men seeking work. State wide, urban areas in J&K have a sex ratio of 822, but in certain districts the figure is shockingly low: below 700 in Leh, Kargil, Doda, and Udhampur districts; and just over 700 in Kupwara and Rajauri.[4]

---

1. Office of the Registrar General, "Provisional Population Totals: India," Census of India 2001, http://www.censusindia.net/results/provindia1.html, accessed June 2, 2003.

2. State Plan Division, Planning Commission, Government of India, *State Development Report: Jammu and Kashmir* [hereafter J&K DR] (New Delhi: Planning Commission, September 2003), pp. 209–219, http://planningcommission.nic.in/plans/stateplan/sdr_jandk/sdr_jandk.htm.

3. Office of the Registrar General, "Provisional Population Totals: India," Census of India 2001.

On the other hand, infant mortality is close to the national average, at 64 per thousand live births, and reported mortality for children under five years old was substantially below the national average, at 80 per thousand, compared with a national figure of 95. Nutrition and access to basic health facilities seem to be significantly better than the national average, with fewer underweight children and more children having been vaccinated and receiving vitamin A supplements.[5] Population per hospital bed is 868, compared to a national average of 1,460.[6] State expenditures on health were among the highest in the country, at 2.72 percent of state domestic product. The states with higher public expenditures on education and health tended to be, like Kashmir, states with troubled politics and a difficult relationship with New Delhi, such as the small states of the Northeast.[7] Health is, of course, not simply a matter of counting providers and facilities. In this regard, Kashmir's highly polluted waterways have left 60 percent of the population without access to clean water, a problem that is made worse by rapid urbanization.[8]

Jammu and Kashmir is the only state in India that has made education free to all its citizens at all levels. Nonetheless, literacy, at 54 percent, lags behind the all-India level of 65 percent. The discrepancy is slightly larger for women (42 percent, compared to the national figure of 54) than for men (66 percent, compared with a national level of 76). The census figures on literacy show stark discrepancies within the state. Except for Srinagar District, the Valley of Kashmir has literacy rates of between 41 and 47 percent, on a par with Bihar, the least literate state in India. In these same districts, female literacy is below 30 percent. On the other hand, Jammu District has a literacy rate of 77 percent, one of the highest in India. There were technical problems with the way these figures were collected in Jammu and Kashmir, but discrepancies this large are worrisome nonetheless.[9]

Government spending on education is relatively generous, in line with the pattern observed elsewhere in this report that the Kashmiri economy is highly dependent on government funds. Official estimates for 1998–1999 show public expenditures on education at 6 percent of state domestic product; the median level in India was just under 4 percent. The number of schools per thousand population was sharply higher than the national average: figures for 2001 show 7.89 primary schools and 4.93 secondary schools, compared to national figures of 5.05 and 2.75 respectively.[10]

---

4. Ibid., cited in J&K DR, p. 35.

5. "National Family Health Survey 2," International Institute for Population Sciences, Mumbai, http://www.nfhsindia.org/data/india/keyfact.pdf. The J&K DR shows a state infant mortality rate of 45, based on the Sample Registration System, but notes that its figures are "not reliable" because of collection problems due to the insurgency.

6. Planning Commission, Government of India, *National Human Development Report 2001* (New Delhi: Planning Commission, March 2002), p. 257, http://planningcommission.nic.in/reports/genrep/reportsf.htm.

7. Ibid., p. 216.

8. See J&K DR, pp. 209–219.

9. Office of the Registrar General, "Literacy Rate: India," Census of India 2001, http://www.censusindia.net/results/provindia3.html, accessed August 18, 2005; see also J&K DR, p. 37. The figures are for population aged 7 and older.

If taken at face value, the state government's figures on teachers and school enrollment suggest an educational system in great trouble. At the primary level, the number of schools remained about the same from 1996 to 1999, but the number of teachers rose by 81 percent and the number of students by 27 percent. At the middle and high school levels, the number of schools rose by 13 and 7 percent respectively, and the number of teachers went up by 18 percent. But the number of students fell sharply: the number of boys in middle school fell by 44 percent; the number of students in high school fell by 24 percent, boys and girls by about the same percentage.[11]

One should be cautious drawing conclusions, especially since the likelihood of flawed statistics is high. Anecdotal evidence and journalistic descriptions suggest that education has been badly disrupted in those districts that are most affected by the insurgency. This could help explain the drop in male high school enrollment, and the concomitant insecurity could reduce female enrollment at the high school level (although there was virtually no change in female enrollment at the middle school level). The sharp increase in the number of primary school teachers suggests that the state government may be hiring teachers as a way to reduce unemployment and perhaps distribute political favors. Overreporting is also a possibility, to convey the impression that social progress is being made. It all suggests that education is a crisis area that needs improved staffing and careful thought to address; simply increasing funding will have little effect.

Growth, Income, and Poverty

In the past two decades, India has enjoyed unprecedented growth, but Jammu and Kashmir has to a large extent been left behind. In the decade from 1980–1981 to 1990–1991, the state domestic product for Jammu and Kashmir grew by only 29.5 percent; the comparable figure for India as a whole was 71.9 percent. During the 1990s, the gap narrowed a bit but was still daunting: 35.8 percent growth in J&K compared with 54.1 percent for India as a whole. That places J&K near the bottom in growth among Indian states.[12]

The Indian Ministry of Finance gives a 2001–2002 estimate of per capita net state product at Rs. 13,320 ($279.29).[13] This is 33 percent below the all-India figure for the same year and represents a significant deterioration since 1993, when J&K's per capita net state product stood 12 percent below the national average.[14]

10. Planning Commission, Government of India, *National Human Development Report 2001*, p. 216.

11. Cited in J&K DR, p. 144.

12. Reserve Bank of India, *Handbook of Statistics on Indian Economy 2001* (Mumbai: Reserve Bank of India, January 2002), pp. 8–17.

13. Dollar figures are computed using the exchange rates for the year in question from Ministry of Finance, Government of India, *Economic Survey of India 2004–2005* (New Delhi: Ministry of Finance, 2005), table 6.5, http://indiabudget.nic.in/es2004-05/chapt2005/tab65.pdf, accessed September 2, 2005.

14. See Ministry of Finance, Government of India, *Economic Survey of India 2004–2005*, table 1.1, http://indiabudget.nic.in/es2004-05/chapt2005/tab11.pdf, accessed September 2, 2005.

Estimates of the percentage of the population below the poverty line differ widely. Government estimates cited in the press go as low as 3 percent. The *Human Development Report* (HDR) estimated the 1983 poverty rate at 30 percent in rural areas and 9 percent in urban areas. A socioeconomic survey conducted in 2004 estimated poverty in two largely rural districts in the Kashmir Valley, Anantnag and Budgam, at 31 percent.[15] Estimates of consumption, however, suggest that the population's living standards may be higher than state's apparent economic stagnation would suggest. The HDR estimates per capita consumption in Kashmir at close to the Indian average in 1983 and 26 percent above the national average in 2000 (39 percent higher for the rural population). Kashmir is even further ahead of the national average for consumption after one adjusts for income inequality in the state and for inflation.[16] Motor vehicle ownership is below the national average,[17] but reports cited in the press suggest that those able to afford land and motor vehicles in Kashmir have increased in number in the past decade. A newspaper account argues that land prices in residential areas rose seven-fold, and in commercial areas ten-fold, during the 1990s.[18] A *New York Times* story states that the number of registered motor vehicles increased by a factor of five and the number of private schools by a factor of three.[19] Bank deposits have surged: the same story reports that deposits in the Jammu and Kashmir Bank grew from $458 million, equivalent to $2.29 billion during the 1990s.[20] Aggregate deposits increased 14 percent, just above the national average, between March 2004 and March 2005.[21] These observations could reflect a high standard of living at least among the urban elite; they could also reflect inflows of "black money" from a variety of sources.

One independent, unpublished study has looked at the question of human security. In this survey, J&K falls at about the mid-point of Indian states, according to a ranking of Indian states derived from figures collected by the central government. The ranking is a composite one and includes a number of measures of violence, infant mortality, disease, and drug abuse.[22]

---

15. Asian Development Bank, "Report and Recommendation to the Board of Directors on a Proposed Loan to India for the Multisector Project for Infrastructure Rehabilitation in Jammu and Kashmir (IND 38136), Manila, December 2004, p. 20.

16. Planning Commission, Government of India, *National Human Development Report 2001*, pp. 147–149.

17. Tata Services Limited, *Statistical Outline of India 2004-5* (Mumbai: Tata Services Limited, 2005), p. 137. Vehicle ownership in J&K in 2002 was 3,519 per 100,000 population, compared to a national figure of 5,617.

18. Murali Krishnan, "A Touch of Unreality," OutlookIndia.com, September 3, 2001.

19. Amy Waldman, "Border Tensions a Growth Industry for Kashmir," *New York Times*, October 18, 2002.

20. Ibid.

21. Jammu and Kashmir Bank, "67th Annual Report," Srinagar, 2005, http://jkbank.net/reports/67annualreport_complete.pdf, accessed August 19, 2005.

22. Unpublished papers prepared by the Human Security in India Project Team, Jawaharlal Nehru University, New Delhi. Shared with the author by Happymon Jacob, Jammu University, March 23, 2005.

Government and the Economy

The explanation for the apparent inconsistencies between sluggish growth and high consumption lies in the state's stormy political history. More than a decade of insurgency, following a much longer period of misgovernance, has created far-reaching distortions and anomalies in the economy. Production of staple crops has done badly, but horticulture has done well; construction is booming; tourism was virtually wiped out for close to a decade, but enjoyed a resurgence starting in 2003; the security presence in the valley depressed certain kinds of economic activity while providing a ready source of income for those who sold goods to the army.

One theme running through this often contradictory story is that of heavy and growing dependence of the Kashmiri economy on government expenditures, at both the state and central level. The controller and auditor general of India calculated that the state government's budget expenditures, both revenue and capital, came to an average of 48 percent of gross state domestic product between 2000 and 2004. The norm in other Indian states is 15 to 20 percent, although the other insurgency-affected states in the northeast have a profile similar to Kashmir. Nearly all of this was revenue (i.e., noncapital) expenditure—an average of 40 percent. Government salary expenditure during these same years was 15 to 21 percent of gross state domestic product; the comparable figures in the states cited above were 4 to 6 percent.[23] By any measure this makes the state economy overwhelmingly dependent on the state government, and it makes state government employment by far the largest nonagricultural source of jobs (an issue that will be discussed in more depth in the section herein on employment).

The dependence on government is even greater when one considers the role of the central government. Official budget figures show central government grants-in-aid as 68 percent of the state government's revenue receipts in 2003–2004. The norm is 4 to 20 percent; again, the insurgency-affected states in the northeast have figures of the same order of magnitude as J&K.[24] Like the northeastern states, J&K is a "special category" state, which means that 90 percent of central government funding is provided on a grant basis, compared to 30 percent for a "normal" state.

Besides its role in financing state government expenditures, the central government maintains a large security presence in J&K and has promised substantial federal funds to Kashmir in an effort to revive normal activity. The Rs. 85,190-million ($1.76-billion) package announced in 2002 included funding for railways, roads, support for traditional handicrafts, support payments to military and police families, raising two additional reserve battalions, support for Hindus who had been forced out of the Kashmir Valley, and economic development in the border areas. Subsequent packages have focused on employment and on the power sector as well. Implementation is moving slowly, but the stated price tag on the package is

---

23. Comptroller and Auditor General of India, *Audit Report: Jammu and Kashmir for the Year 2003–2004*, http://cag.nic.in/, pp. 10–11, accessed August 26, 2005. Figures for other states are from the same Web site.

24. Ibid., p. 5.

enormous: it exceeds the total state government noncapital expenditures for 2003–2004.[25]

The state government's management of its funds makes its predominant economic position all the more worrisome. The current state planning authorities are trying to reduce the state's dependence on deficit financing, but it is difficult to reconcile their statements of "zero deficit budgets" with the published figures. The controller and auditor general's report estimates the state's fiscal liabilities at Rs. 130,380 million in 2004—over 150 percent of total annual state expenditures, and 63 percent of gross state domestic product. The state government used a combination of "ways and means advances" and overdrafts from the Jammu and Kashmir Bank to finance its operations. The overdraft facility was used every day of the year in 2003–2004. The total overdrafts taken during the year exceeded that year's total expenditures, and the amount remaining at the end of the year stood at Rs. 15,465 million ($336.55 million). By way of comparison, none of the states cited above used their overdraft facility for more than 160 days during the year, and the percentage of total expenditures never exceeded 22 percent.[26] Doubts about the management of state government funds are intensified by the conclusion of a study by Transparency International India and the Centre for Media Studies that rates J&K as the second most corrupt Indian state, after Bihar. Countrywide, the police are rated by the same study as the most corrupt government service, something that has particular weight in Kashmir given the unsettled security situation and people's frequent interactions with the police.[27]

Employment—and Unemployment

J&K has a work force of some 4.4 million or 44 percent of its population. Of these, the Indian Planning Commission's *Jammu and Kashmir Development Report* shows 70 percent employed in agriculture, very close to the national average.[28] Not surprisingly, dependence on agriculture is lowest in the more heavily urbanized Srinagar and Jammu districts (40 and 48 percent respectively) and much higher (generally between 65 and 77 percent) in more rural districts. Animal husbandry, forestry, fishing, and orchard keeping add another 3 percentage points to this total.

As for nonagricultural employment, the Jammu and Kashmir state government is overwhelmingly the largest employer, especially for educated workers. Some 20 percent of the state's work force is employed by the state government. Within the

25. Department of Information and Public Relations, Government of Jammu and Kashmir, "Status Report on Implementation of J&K Packages," http://jammukashmir.nic.in/jk.pdf, accessed August 29, 2005.

26. Comptroller and Auditor General of India, *Audit Report: Jammu and Kashmir for the Year 2003–2004*, pp. 1, 17, 18, accessed August 26, 2005. Figures for other states are from the same Web site.

27. Centre for Media Studies, *India Corruption Study 2005: To Improve Governance* (New Delhi: Transparency International India, June 2005), http://www.cmsindia.org/cms/events/corruption.pdf, accessed August 29, 2005.

28. J&K DR, p. 43.

state government, education and law enforcement each employ about one-third of the total.[29] Outside the government sector, manufacturing, primarily handicrafts, accounts for the largest single share of employment, 11.2 percent, with "household manufacturing" accounting for half of this. The other significant fields for employment are construction (2.8 percent), trade and commerce (5.6 percent), and other services.

Unemployment figures are notoriously unreliable in countries with a large agricultural work force. The *Human Development Report* prepared by the Indian government estimates that employment grew by 1.1 percent between 1993 and 1999, less than half of population growth.[30] The comparable figure for India as a whole is 1.6 percent, compared with a much smaller population growth. Among those registered with the state employment exchange, the number of educated job seekers grew by 48 percent during the 1990s, from 112,000 to 167,000, whereas the number of illiterate job seekers fell by 28 percent.[31] Another estimate cited in Gupta shows unemployment at just over 10 percent of the work force from 1985 to 1991.[32] This must be considered a bare minimum figure, especially when one considers the near certainty of underemployment due to falling agricultural output and sharply rising state government expenditures whose output is unclear. Another study claims that unemployment in 1998 stood at 700,000, equal to some 18 percent of the workforce, with educated unemployment at 200,000.[33]

Unemployment on this scale is corrosive to a society, especially one that has seen so many of its young people give up on the system and become involved in militancy. A peaceful future for Kashmir will depend critically on the creation of real jobs, in productive sectors of the economy, to mobilize young people for a peaceful future. Thus for reasons of both economics and social soundness, employment needs to be a central feature of any economic plan for the area. Successive governments have implicitly recognized this by making employment creation central to aspects of the development schemes they have developed for Kashmir. The dominant role of government in the state's employment picture, however, has the unfortunate side effect that for many Kashmiris, government jobs are looked on as the only "real" jobs, because of the employment security that the government usually provides.

---

29. Arun Varma, "Economic Development," in *Jammu and Kashmir: An Agenda for the Future,* ed. Kanti Bajpai et al. (New Delhi: Policy Group, 1999), p. 34.

30. Planning Commission, Government of India, *National Human Development Report 2001,* p. 158.

31. J&K DR, pp. 110–112.

32. S.P. Gupta, *Population Growth and the Problem of Un-employment* (New Delhi: Anmol Publications, 1990), pp. 322, 323.

33. Sundeep Waslekar and Ilmas Futehally, *Reshaping the Agenda in Kashmir* (Mumbai: International Centre for Peace Initiatives, 2002), p. 38.

Infrastructure

Power

The Indus and several of its major tributaries flow through Jammu and Kashmir, and the government of India estimates the state's hydroelectric potential at 20,000 megawatts (MW), a resource that ought to be an asset for the state's development. There are no public estimates yet of earthquake damage to electric power infrastructure, but it is reasonable to assume that it was significant.

Current installed hydroelectric generating capacity within the state comes to 1,470 MW. Of this amount, 1,170 MW comes from two major national projects, at Salal and Uri, from which J&K's entitlement comes to 34 percent, with the rest allocated to other parts of India. In addition, the state has 183 MW of thermal generation capacity; this is used primarily to back up the hydro plants, especially during the winter when river flows fall.[34]

Electricity consumption in 2001 was estimated at 3,397 million kilowatt-hours (kWh), up 32 percent from 1997–1998. Net generation from inside the state was estimated at 990 million kWh in 2002. However, transmission and distribution losses come to 46 percent of total available energy. The result is that the state purchased 5,449 million kWh from India's Northern Grid. Internally generated electricity thus represented only 15 percent of the available energy.[35]

The electricity sector in India is the responsibility of the various state electricity boards, all of which have been in financial difficulty. A countrywide rating exercise conducted by the Indian Ministry of Power ranked the J&K State Electricity Board second from last among all the Indian states. The ranking system took into account both technical and financial parameters; J&K's poor showing was based primarily on its very weak financial picture.[36]

Heavy energy purchases and the poor finances of the J&K Electricity Board have contributed heavily to the state government's precarious finances, outlined above. Operating losses (including subsidies) for the Jammu and Kashmir Power Development Department grew from Rs. 3,630 million ($101.2 million) in 1996–1997 to Rs. 9,210 million ($189.6 million) in 2001–2002.[37] According to state government figures, 97 percent of Kashmiri villages are electrified, at least in principle, compared with 86 percent nationwide, and although overall power use per capita is below the national average, the discrepancy is not dramatic (283 kWh compared with a nationwide figure of 360 kWh).[38] Electricity metering is planned but not yet fully implemented, and collections are unreliable. Power outages are commonplace,

---

34. J&K DR, pp. xxxiii, 116, and 118.

35. Power and Energy Division, Planning Commission, Government of India, *Annual Report on the Working of State Electricity Boards and Electricity Departments* (New Delhi: Planning Commission, June 2001) and Power Development Corporation, J&K, June 2002, cited in J&K DR, pp. 118–120.

36. Ministry of Power, Government of India, "Rationale for Jammu & Kashmir State Power Sector Scoring," http://powermin.nic.in/reports/pdf/jammu%20&%20kashmir.pdf, accessed September 2, 2005.

37. Ministry of Power, Government of India, "Power Sector Profile: Northern Region," October 2005, http://powermin.nic.in/indian_electricity_scenario/pdf/NR01005.pdf.

so the actual availability of electricity to Kashmiris is considerably less than these encouraging figures would suggest.

The state has enacted a State Electricity Regulatory Commission Act, which should provide the basis for rationalizing tariffs, unbundling transmission and distribution, introducing private participation into distribution, and other measures for restoring commercial viability and reducing system losses. Implementation of the act's provisions is not yet complete.[39]

The state's huge hydroelectric capacity and its large bill for electricity generated outside the state make a strong case for expanding generation. The state government has been pressing for building major new power plants, and the government of India has undertaken to finance some of the proposals. Government documents and the state government Web site carry long lists of projects under construction or for which bidding is under way. The major installations under consideration, if implemented, would total 4,448 MW in capacity. Many of the largest and best-known projects have been plagued by multi-decade delays and enormous cost overruns. There is considerable potential for small power plants, which would avoid some of the treaty problems described below; the bidding document on the state government's Web site, for example, lists 12 projects totaling 67 MW of capacity.

A more complicated issue arises from the Indus Waters Treaty, signed in 1960 to divide the waters of the six rivers of the Indus system between India and Pakistan. The three rivers awarded to Pakistan flow first through J&K. Under the treaty, India—including J&K—is permitted only "nonconsumptive" use of their water, with carefully crafted restrictions on any structure that stores water, including power plants. In general, this treaty has been the most successful agreement settling any dispute between India and Pakistan, but disagreements have arisen over potential large hydroelectric installations in Kashmir and are likely to intensify in the coming years. Pakistan is one of the most water-short countries in the world, and on this issue its economic interests diverge from those of Kashmir. Pakistan has initiated the treaty's dispute-settlement provisions with respect to the power plant the Indian government has started building at Baglihar (450 MW). If the Indian or J&K authorities proceed with the proposed dam on the Kishenganga river (330 MW), the dispute-settlement process is likely to come into play again even more quickly.

Transportation

Roads are the key means of transportation within the state. Earthquake damage to the road network is extensive and affects both major highways and smaller local roads.

The density of J&K's road network is low by national standards: 6.09 kilometers per 100 square kilometers of area, compared to a national figure of 74; or, put another way, 134 kilometers per 100,000 people, compared with a national figure of

---

38. Directorate of Economics and Statistics, Government of Jammu and Kashmir, *Digest of Statistics 2001-02* (Srinagar: Directorate of Economics and Statistics, 2002), p. 436.

39. J&K DR, p. 120.

245. Given the mountainous terrain in much of the state, these figures are not surprising. Militancy has affected road transport particularly severely, with many explosions aimed at bridges and culverts.[40] In addition, special security measures are in effect for vehicular traffic entering the state. All truck traffic is inspected at a single checkpoint on the road, causing bottlenecks and inevitably creating opportunities for truck operators to be harassed.[41]

Only Jammu is linked by rail to the rest of India. The Indian Railways have plans to extend the line to Udhampur and Srinagar by 2007, but it is uncertain whether this goal will be met. Thus, shipment of goods between India and most of J&K beyond Jammu, including the entire valley, is slow and expensive.[42]

There is civilian air service to Srinagar, Jammu, and Leh, though all three airports are owned by the military. None of them is currently an international airport, so both tourists and cargo need to come through Delhi or other cities in India. Srinagar has some experience with international operations because direct flights for the hajj, or Muslim pilgrimage, do operate from Srinagar. International airport status is a longstanding request of the Srinagar business community,[43] and the government of India has begun planning to designate Srinagar airport as an international airport, possibly as early as 2006. The redesignation is part of a major airport expansion, which would increase its capacity from four to six aircraft at a time and would add substantial capacity for handling both domestic and international passengers.[44] The changes in the airport seem to be primarily designed for handling people rather than cargo; our recommendations herein address this issue.

Communication

Tele-density in J&K in 2001 was about half that in India as a whole: 1.65 connections per 100 people, compared to just over 3 nation wide. The telecommunications department had a list of over 40,000 customers waiting for a land line, equal to about 25 percent of working land connections.[45]

The time since then has been a period of very high growth in telecommunications for India; the number of telephones quadrupled between 1999 and 2004. Cellular service in J&K was banned for years out of concern that militants would take advantage of it. In 2003, the government authorized the largest of the three government-owned cellular phone operators to offer service in the state.[46] However,

---

40. Ibid., pp. 128–137.

41. Author's conversation with members of the Srinagar Chamber of Commerce, Srinagar, March 2004.

42. J&K DR, pp. 128–137; see also Department of Information and Public Relations, Government of Jammu and Kashmir, "Status Report on Implementation of J&K Packages."

43. Author's conversation with members of the Srinagar Chamber of Commerce, Srinagar, March 2004.

44. Press Trust of India, "Srinagar Airport Likely to Be Declared International," *Hindustan Times*, May 9, 2005, http://www.hindustantimes.com/news/181_1354757,000600030010.htm.

45. J&K DR, pp. 140–141.

46. "Kashmiris Snap Up Cell Phones," BBC News, August 18, 2003, http://news.bbc.co.uk/2/hi/south_asia/ 3159905.stm.

service is unreliable, and cellular phones that work in J&K do not work in other parts of India and vice versa. In other words, though communications technology has been introduced, the state is still being kept separate from the rest of India—and from a globalizing world. In other parts of India, wireless phones have now passed land lines as the dominant form of telecommunications. That mechanism for economic acceleration is out of reach for Kashmiris at present.

Major Economic Sectors

Kashmir has a predominantly agricultural economy, but over the past 10 years, as in the rest of India, agriculture has fallen as a percentage of the economy. The Indian government estimates that 24 percent of the state's domestic product derived from agriculture in 2001–2002 and 29 percent from the primary sector as a whole, down from 26 and 33 percent respectively in 1993–1994. The big increases, during the same period, have been in the share of the state's economy from public administration (up from 10 to 16 percent), and in transportation and communication (from 4.6 to 7.7 percent). The share of manufacturing in state product has fallen by nearly half, from 7.8 to 4.7 percent.[47]

Agriculture

Kashmir implemented a major land reform program in 1948–1952. Current figures on land holdings still reflect the results: 52 percent of land holdings in the state are below 0.5 hectares, and 92 percent are below 2 hectares. There are fewer than 200 holdings of over 20 acres.[48] The political benefits, as one might expect, included a surge in political support for the government that instituted the reforms. Through the years, the small holdings that resulted grew smaller still.

Because horticultural land was exempted from the reforms, this created a strong incentive to reconsolidate land and devote it to saffron, orchard crops, and other horticultural products for which Kashmir is famous.[49] One side effect of this shift of resources into horticulture is greater dependence on the outside world for basic food grains. In purely income terms, however, this is probably good economic strategy for J&K—an example of comparative advantage at work.

The 1990s saw a drop in food grain production. The Reserve Bank of India's annual report for 2001 estimated that food grain production had stagnated at 1.3 million to 1.5 million metric tons during the 1990s and fallen to 0.8 million in 2000.[50] The fall affected all major crops, most importantly rice and wheat. Agricultural output is highly variable however. The year 2001–2002 saw gains in wheat

---

47. Ministry of Statistics and Program Implementation, Government of India, "Jammu & Kashmir: Gross State Domestic Product," http://mospi.nic.in/rept%20_%20pubn/ftest.asp?rept_id=nad03_1993_1994 &type=NSSO.

48. Directorate of Economics and Statistics, Government of Jammu and Kashmir, *Digest of Statistics 2001-02*, p. 80.

49. Well-informed observers argue that this has been an important trend; the state's *Digest of Statistics* shows 72,000 hectares, or about 7 percent of area under agricultural production, being devoted to horticultural production, a percentage that has risen only slightly over the past decade.

production to 0.34 million metric tons with a yield of 1,325 kilograms per hectare as compared to 0.15 million metric tons and a yield of 529 kilograms per hectare in 2000–2001.[51]

Horticulture has apparently done better, though the earthquake may have destroyed as much as a quarter of the Kashmiri apple crop, probably including many standing trees.[52] The total area under cultivation for fruits and vegetables stood at 66,000 hectares in 1999–2000.[53] Anecdotal evidence suggests that horticulture has been relatively little affected by militants or security operations. Some 95 percent of horticultural acreage is in the Kashmir Valley. Production of the four major crops—apples, pears, walnuts, and almonds—topped 1 million metric tons in 2001–2002. Cherries, apricots, plums, strawberries, and grapes are coming up as well. The state's planning authorities estimate the annual output of the saffron industry at Rs. 5,000 million per year ($104.84 million) and the value of the overall horticulture sector at about Rs. 15,000 million per year ($314.52 million).[54] Nearly 75 percent of the tonnage of major horticultural crops is sold outside the state. Horticulture is an important source of employment as well as income; the Planning Commission estimates that each hectare of production generates 500 person-days of jobs per year and that 500,000 families derive their livelihood from horticulture.[55]

Kashmir is known for silk production. The number of mulberry trees in the state nearly doubled between 1980 and 2000, but the trees have not survived well and the productivity of the industry has been uneven. The value of silk production has stagnated since 1996, and the number of households dependent on sericulture was estimated at about 25,000 in 2000, down from 38,500 in 1980.[56]

Many observers believe the horticultural economy could do much better with the introduction of an even greater variety of high value crops, such as medicinal herbs, mushrooms, and crops with niche markets inside or outside the region. Greater investment in sophisticated packaging and processing facilities is also badly needed. Little processing takes place in the state. The state government's investment incentive package cites horticulture as a key industry, and both the central and state governments' plans include improvements in transportation between J&K and the rest of India that would further boost the profitability of the horticulture sector. J&K faces competition in this sector from Himachal Pradesh, which has a similar climate, can produce many of the same crops, and has better transportation links to

50. Reserve Bank of India, *Handbook of Statistics on Indian Economy 2001*, p. 35. The Directorate of Economics and Statistics, *Digest of Statistics*, shows a similar trend.

51. Ministry of Agriculture, Government of India, "Agricultural Statistics at a Glance 2003," http://agricoop.nic.in/statistics2003/chap4a.htm#chap47, accessed August 18, 2005.

52. Aijaz Hussain, "Kashmir Quake: India's Disaster—Deadly Delay," *India Today*, October 17, 2005.

53. Ministry of Agriculture, Government of India, "Agricultural Statistics at a Glance 2003," http://agricoop.nic.in/statistics2003/chap5.htm#chap57.

54. Mandavi Mehta conversation with Vijay Bakaya, planning secretary, J&K government, August 2003; Gautam Navlakha, "Political Economy of Fiscal Autonomy," *Greater Kashmir*, July 30, 2003.

55. J&K DR, pp. 287–297.

56. "Statistical Abstract 1999–2000," Government of J&K, cited in J&K DR, pp. 82–85.

the main Indian markets. Kashmir's unsettled security situation remains the major obstacle to taking full advantage of its potential. The security picture discourages investors and scares off banks, which have been burned by bad loans in the past.

Forests are a major resource in J&K, with over 20,000 square forested kilometers. Half of the area of the Kashmir region is under forests and 45 percent of the Jammu region. Most of the forest resources are coniferous soft woods (18,345 square kilometers). State government figures show significant but falling revenues from forests, substantial but falling figures for the overall amount of forest products produced (162,000 cubic meters in 2001–2002).[57] Exports of forest products are estimated at 11,000 cubic meters in 2001–2002.[58]

These figures do not reflect the massive illegal harvesting of timber that is widely reported to be taking place, in some cases with the cooperation of security forces. Ecologists fear that Kashmir's natural heritage is being destroyed. The problem is especially acute in Ladakh, where the high-altitude, arid ecosystem is particularly fragile. Preserving and restoring forest resources needs to be a central objective of an effort to find economic peace builders in the state.

Handicrafts

Kashmir is famous for carpet weaving and knotting, namdas (wool and cotton floor coverings and wall hangings), papier mâché, chain stitch and crewel fabrics, shawls, basketry, walnut wood carving, and copper and silver work. The most important sector is carpets, which accounts for 25 percent of employment in handicrafts and over 80 percent of the value of production. State government figures estimate that 320,000 people worked in the handicraft sector in 2001–2002. Many handicraft workers have traditionally been children; not surprisingly, there are no figures documenting the extent of child labor. Government figures estimate handicraft production at Rs. 633 million ($13.27 million) and exports worth Rs. 504 million ($10.57 million).[59] Private estimates run as much as 10 times that level.[60]

Industry

The industrial sector in J&K is plagued with problems. The share of manufacturing in J&K state domestic product is well below the national average and has fallen during the period of the insurgency. Most of the state's industrial capacity is in the Jammu region, which is more favorably situated and has better transportation links to the rest of India. In addition, in recent years, the security situation in the Kashmir Valley has drastically curtailed activity outside the home after dark. The result is that industries can only operate one shift.[61]

---

57. Directorate of Economics and Statistics, Government of Jammu and Kashmir, *Digest of Statistics 2001-02*, pp. 107–109.

58. Ibid.

59. Ibid., pp. 179–181; J&K DR, pp. 314–316.

60. Author's correspondence with former president of J&K Bank, M.Y. Khan, who estimates handicraft sales outside J&K at over Rs. 5 billion, including carpet sales of over Rs. 3 billion.

61. Author's conversation with members of the Srinagar Chamber of Commerce, Srinagar, March 2004.

Industrial employment was estimated by the state government at 187,000 in 2000–2001, having risen slowly but steadily in the preceding five years. Industrial output has been volatile, falling by over half between 1995–1996 and 1997–1998, and recovering about half that lost ground by 2000–2001, when it was estimated at Rs. 2179 million ($47.7million). Financing approved for industrial enterprises large enough to deal with the formal financial sector has grown during this period, but loans actually disbursed have fallen fairly steadily, from Rs. 135 million ($2.96 million) to Rs. 98 million ($2.15 million).[62] These figures are consistent with the report from individual business people that using credit on normal commercial terms—or even on somewhat concessional terms—is a very risky proposition in the current business climate in Kashmir.[63]

The state government runs a number of agencies to promote and assist industry, including the J&K State Industrial Corporation Ltd. (SIDCO), oriented toward medium- and large-scale industry; the J&K Small Scale Industries Development Corporation (SICOP), for the development of small-scale industry; the Small Industries Service Institute (SISI), a technical support organization; and the State Financial Corporation, which has become a major source of industrial financing, nearly equaling the loans provided by the principal local commercial bank, Jammu and Kashmir Bank, in 2000–2001. The two industrial support agencies and the state government's Department of Industries and Commerce maintain a total of 50 industrial estates, which are home to 968 functioning industrial units. These are not export processing zones (EPZs), but simply areas set up to provide the infrastructure needed by an industrial operation.[64]

There is at least one EPZ in Jammu and an additional one is planned for Srinagar. The existing EPZ does not seem to have been very effective. Studies from many countries have shown that new investment is much more heavily influenced by the basic investment climate than by the kinds of tax incentives incorporated in an EPZ.

The state government also owns some 20 industrial units, ranging from hand-loom development and horticultural marketing and processing to power development. Only five of these public-sector units are operating in the black, and those five, in the construction, tourism, cable car, forestry, and cement businesses, are just breaking even. The loss-making public-sector units are a further drain on the state government's budget, from which they draw support. The state has considered privatization or disinvestment but not surprisingly has had little success with either.[65]

Both the state government and the central government have put in place a variety of incentives for industry in J&K. Capital subsidies, exemption from tolls and sales tax, and preferences in procurement by the state government are standard mechanisms, but they are unlikely to make much difference until investors are reassured about their basic business prospects and the security situation.

62. J&K DR, pp. 95–96.
63. Author's conversations with members of the Srinagar Chamber of Commerce, Srinagar, February 26, 2004.
64. J&K DR, pp. 96–100.
65. Ibid., pp. 96–102.

Internationally, there tends to be a lag between improvements in basic security and the restoration of business confidence, so this will be a slow process. The state government has also put in place huge subsidies for air freight, research and development, and training costs.[66] These could make a difference once the basic security questions have been resolved, but they will be a considerable drain on the state budget.

There has also been much talk about establishing industries based on information technology (IT), since this type of industry is less vulnerable than manufacturing to security disruptions, and IT-based industries can function well in remote locations provided the telecommunications infrastructure is adequate. But in general, businesses that are establishing IT-based facilities have easier options available to them than Kashmir, and broadband and cellular phone service is substantially worse in J&K than elsewhere in India.

As security improves, the business community in J&K may have more success in attracting investment from Indian IT companies. A software technology park was established in Rangreth, Srinagar, in January 2001, with central government assistance. It moved very slowly for three years. The India-Pakistan cease-fire in late 2003 and the decision to begin liberalizing access to cellular phones and broadband communications seem to have broken the ice. By the summer of 2004, the park had four functioning companies, including one jointly owned by a nonresident Kashmiri and an American entrepreneur. They were still delivering most of their work in physical form (on paper or on CDs) rather than by electronic communications.[67]

Tourism

Scenery is perhaps the most famous resource of J&K, and tourism was for decades a pillar of the local economy. According to state government estimates, up to 30 percent of the state population directly or indirectly benefits from it, and it contributes 16 percent to the state's domestic product.[68]

Tourism has been particularly hard hit by insecurity in the state and by the related inconvenience of travel through the intrusive security measures at Srinagar airport. In 1988, before the insurgency became serious, 722,000 tourists visited the Kashmir Valley, of whom 60,000, or about 8 percent, came from outside India. During the 1990s, the number of visitors fluctuated wildly, with lows of about 8,000 during several years in the mid-1990s and in 2002, and much higher figures (100,000–250,000) in the late 1990s and again in 2003 and 2004.[69] This volatility has taken its toll on the facilities that support the tourism industry, with many hotels

---

66.   Jammu and Kashmir Government, "Salient Features of J&K Industrial Policy 2004," http://jammukashmir.nic.in/govt/SFIP2004.pdf, accessed August 18, 2005.

67.   J&K DR, p. 106; Altaf Hussain, "Kashmir Logs on to IT Boom," BBC News, August 12, 2004, http://news.bbc.co.uk/2/hi/south_asia/3554914.stm, accessed September 9, 2005.

68.   Planning and Development Department, Government of Jammu and Kashmir, "Draft Ninth Five-Year Plan, 1997–2002," cited in J&K DR, p. 329. Note that these figures include indirect benefits and would thus include employment and income generated in the transportation, handicraft, and many other sectors.

69.   J&K DR, pp. 329–335.

falling into disrepair and owners reluctant to incur debt—even assuming they can find financing—in order to maintain facilities whose profitability is so fragile.

Kashmir boasts three other major tourist destinations: Ladakh and Hindu holy places in Amarnath and Vaishnodevi. The number of pilgrims has been somewhat less volatile, although there were periods when pilgrims were attacked by militants.[70] Winter tourism has tremendous potential, largely undeveloped. Mountaineering, ecotourism, and other specialized forms of tourism would also be an attractive industry to build up. They would attract a relatively small number of people, but the per-visitor profit could be large. Sites in the Pir Panjal mountains in Jammu, on the other hand, could attract larger numbers of visitors.

Trade outside the State, and Remittances

Horticulture, handicrafts, and forest products are Kashmir's principal export products. Interestingly, Kashmir's out-of-state and export trade seems to have benefited in unexpected ways from the security problems of the last decade. Traditional distribution channels depended on non-Kashmiri brokers who traveled to Kashmir, extended credit to producers of horticultural products and crafts, and marketed goods around India. With violent conditions in the Kashmir Valley, the brokers were reluctant to travel, and Kashmiris moved into the brokering business, capturing more of the value added and providing a better return to producers in the process.[71]

International Assistance

Until quite recently, India did not permit foreign aid agencies to operate in J&K. In 2004, it changed this policy to permit operations by multilateral development institutions, and the Asian Development Bank approved the first foreign-funded project there in two decades. Bilateral donors, however, are still not allowed to operate in J&K. The involvement of both bilateral and multilateral aid agencies, together with improved security, could boost investment and consequently make a dent in the region's severe unemployment problem.

The government of India normally does not accept foreign assistance for disaster relief, and this seems to apply to the Kashmir earthquake as well. Following other natural disasters, India has accepted aid for reconstruction, however.

Economics and Security

The insecurity that has plagued Kashmir for decades, but especially since 1989, has affected the economic and social life of the state in many ways. We will examine three issues: the refugee problem; issues affecting women; and "conflict entrepre-

---

70. Ibid.

71. Author's conversation with Wajahat Habibullah, former chief secretary of Kashmir, February 2004; conversations with members of the Srinagar Chamber of Commerce, Srinagar, February 2004.

neurship" (the question of who profits from the current situation and might therefore be a hidden obstacle to its amelioration).

Refugees and the Pandit Community

The Hindu Pandit community, traditionally a prominent part of society in the Valley of Kashmir, has been devastated by the violence since 1989. The Indian Census of 1981 counted 123,900 Hindus living in the Kashmir region of J&K. The vast majority left the valley in the 1990s, as a result both of general violence and of attacks on their community. Most of those still living in J&K are in refugee camps in the Jammu region, while the majority of those who left are in Delhi or elsewhere in India, living either in camps or with relatives. The numbers for this exodus are hotly disputed. Based on the limited census figures that are available from 2001, a number close to 100,000 seems most likely. Pandit publications say that there are 140,000 registered Pandit refugees in Jammu.[72] The central government has made camps available and has funded the payment of a special allowance of Rs. 850 per month (about $20) per migrant, up to a total of four per family, through the state governments in the places where the refugees are located.[73]

Life has been tough for the few Pandits who remained in Kashmir. One Pandit organization asserts that there were 24,000 Pandits employed in the state government before 1990 but that this number is now down to 3,000. The state government has no budget for compensation for Pandit victims of violence. There have been court cases over standards for state government compensation for destroyed houses; the Pandits believe that the state compensates Muslims more generously than non-Muslims. They complain of discrimination in the job market. And of course the problem of violence continues. Militant organizations have at various times made a point of targeting the few remaining Pandits.

Pandits living outside the valley very much want to return home, not just as individuals but as a community. Doing so would require a complex package of political, social, and economic arrangements for which no preparations have been made at this time.

Women

The situation of women in J&K and its impact on the economy is not well captured by economic statistics. Like both India and Pakistan, J&K has a traditional culture in which women have not historically had a major role in the formal economy. Women were present in the nationalist movement from the early days. As happens in many conflict-torn societies, they have assumed a more public voice in the period since 1989, as politically active men or men involved in the insurgency have been arrested or otherwise prevented from participating in public life. At the same

---

72. Office of the Registrar General, "Jammu and Kashmir, Household Population by Religion of Head of Household, up to Tehsil and Town Level," Census of India 1981; and Office of the Registrar General, "First Report on Religion," Census of India 2001. Kashmiri Pandit organizations, notably the All India Kashmir Samaj, cite figures up to 350,000, of which 200,000 are said to be in Jammu, 100,000 in Delhi, and the rest in other parts of India.

73. N.K. Kaw, president, All India Kashmiri Samaj, conversation with author, March 19, 2005.

time, conservative Islamic organizations have tried to push women back into the home. Periods when militants used threats or violence to enforce a conservative dress code have alternated with periods when women were quite visible embodiments of protest.

A decade and a half of violence in Kashmir has left many women widowed—at least 25,000, according to press reports. It has also created a significant population of "half widows," women whose husbands have disappeared but have not been confirmed dead. Official figures estimate 4,000; the Association of Parents of Disappeared Persons estimates 8,000 to 10,000. The economic role of women has clearly increased during this period, especially in families where men were either involved in the insurgency or cut off from their normal livelihood. At the same time, their social and economic vulnerability has increased.[74]

Women's rights have also been something of a political football in state politics. The state legislature was persuaded with some difficulty in early 2005 to withdraw a measure that would have deprived Kashmiri women of their property rights as residents of Kashmir if they married outside the state.[75]

Winners and Losers

Fifteen years of violence takes a toll on a society, but it also creates its own set of winners. Those who would build peace, through whatever combination of political or economic means, must take into consideration the interests created and nurtured by the dynamic of conflict.

Those who suffer from the continuing violence and unresolved political problem are easy to identify. They include much of the general, job-creating business community; those civilians, military, police, and insurgents whose lives or health are threatened by violence; and young people looking for an education or a stable, legitimate career. Conversations about the future in the Kashmir Valley all include the rueful observation that talented young people are trying to leave. Normal, lawful government processes also suffer.

But there are also many who have figured out how to profit from the conflict, either literally or figuratively. One piece of evidence that some people in the Kashmir Valley have plenty of money comes from the booming construction industry. Any number of anecdotal accounts describe it; the road to Srinagar airport is sprouting grand new houses; and carpenters and other artisans are said to be busy as never before.[76]

Some of those who benefit from the current situation are legitimate businesses and law-abiding individuals: those who sell goods to the military and police; laborers who are building the fence along the Line of Control between Indian and Pakistani forces; suppliers of guard and security services; local businesses who have

---

74. For a much fuller explanation of this process, see Kavita Suri, "Women in the Valley: From Victims to Agents of Change," in *Kashmir: New Voices*, ed. W.P.S. Sidhu (Boulder, Colo.: Lynne Rienner, forthcoming).

75. Luv Puri, "All Kashmir Women to Get Permanent Resident Status," *The Hindu*, February 16, 2005.

76. Author's observations and conversations with recent travelers to Srinagar; and Waldman, "Border Tensions a Growth Industry for Kashmir."

taken over functions once performed by outsiders who no longer wish to come to Kashmir under present circumstances. Most of these people's interests can be accommodated through an economic approach that enhances employment and business security.

But other "winners" from the war are basically making a profit from activities that are either illegal or outside the boundaries of socially acceptable economic behavior. These include political parties and organizations that are being paid off by governments trying to manipulate Kashmiri politics; insurgents paid by one side, and sometimes by both, to keep the conflict going or to manage it in some way; businesses that provide cover for illegal financial transactions; and government officials, civilian and military, who use their position and the security situation to extort money from local citizens. The long history of intelligence operations by both India and Pakistan in Kashmir has created a tolerance for corruption and in some cases an incentive to engage in it for the governments of both Pakistan and India, as well as for the state government. Because these activities are widespread, illegal, and unacknowledged, they are especially hard to root out. The temptation is always strong to pull one more string or enjoy one more payoff. It is perhaps not surprising that a recent study by Transparency International and the Center for Media Studies ranked J&K the second most corrupt state in India, after Bihar.[77]

Uneven Development: Other Parts of J&K

This discussion of the economy in J&K has treated it as one unit. In reality, the economic situation differs from region to region and to some extent from district to district. The areas most severely affected by the insurgency are the six districts of the Kashmir region and the three districts of the Jammu region that have Muslim majorities (Doda, Poonch, and Rajauri). While district-by-district economic statistics are spotty and often unreliable, it is reasonable to assume that these are the districts that have suffered most from declining agricultural and industrial production, uncertain finances, and the disruption of social economic activity that comes from frequent curfews, violent incidents, and other manifestations of the insurgency. These same districts have been the primary target of economic rehabilitation packages announced by both the central and the state governments.

The rest of Jammu, closer to the rest of India and served by a rail line, has distinct advantages when it comes to producing industrial goods and transporting products for sale to states to the south. Residents of the valley complain that the central government's normal development programs are primarily spent in Jammu. Residents of Jammu observe that they have a hard time getting benefits from supposedly statewide rehabilitation programs.

---

77. Center for Media Studies, *India Corruption Study 2005: To Improve Governance* (New Delhi: Transparency International, June 2005), http://www.cmsindia.org/cms/events/corruption.pdf.

Ladakh faces the most severe economic constraints. Its land area is huge and sparsely populated, its climate is harsh, water is scarce, and rainfall rare. It is also relatively inaccessible, with the land connections open only about five months out of the year. A number of sensitive military outposts, notably those on the Siachen and Baltoro glaciers, are in Ladakh. As long as the present political status quo continues, Ladakh is likely to remain highly dependent on the military. Army personnel make up a sizable portion of Ladakh's population and an even larger share of the region's collective purchasing power.

The Kashmir, Jammu, and Ladakh regions also have very different attitudes toward the issue of autonomy from the government in Delhi. For most Muslims of the Kashmir Valley, creating political distance from Delhi is critical, and the process of building peace constituencies through economic means includes empowering local people to make their own economic decisions. For residents of Jammu and Ladakh, the connection with Delhi is valued for its own sake and as a way to avoid being dominated by the Muslims of the valley. Consequently, the "autonomy" issue with greatest salience to them is preserving and enhancing their ability to function independently of the Kashmir Valley. Even within these broad regions, there are significant differences in perspective, with Muslim majority areas in both Jammu and Ladakh concerned to maintain their own identity and voice, distinct from the Hindu majority in Jammu and the Buddhist majority in Ladakh.

The state government is looked on with some degree of skepticism in all three regions: for the valley Muslims, it is too close to Delhi; for the other two groups, it is an instrument of domination by the valley. An economic program intended to build peace constituencies will need to be sensitive to the different interests of these distinct groups in J&K, as well as to the divergent needs on the Pakistan side of the Line of Control, which we address in the next section of this report.

CHAPTER 3

The Pakistani Side: Azad Kashmir and the Northern Areas

The Pakistani-controlled area of Kashmir includes Azad ("Free") Kashmir and the Northern Areas, comprising the divisions of Gilgit and Baltistan. These areas are governed separately, and their populations differ in language, religion, and history. The Northern Areas have the most recent connection with the old princely state and the most limited interaction with the rest of the state.

Azad Kashmir

Azad Jammu and Kashmir (AJK) is mountainous, with small scattered communities and few major urban centers. It has no railway system. The area has little or no industrial base and is predominantly rural. The terrain, level of poverty, and other conditions vary according to the region. Moving south from Muzaffarabad, the area under cultivation increases and becomes more accessible from Pakistan.[1] With marginal agriculture and little industry, the region is unusually dependent on migration, both to the rest of Pakistan and overseas.

The earthquake of October 8, 2005, was centered in AJK and left at least 70,000 dead and 74,000 injured in AJK and adjoining areas of Pakistan. The discussion of the earthquake at the beginning of this report described the immediate impact on AJK and its capital, Muzaffarabad. Relief operations are continuing as this report goes to press. The region affected by the earthquake was for the most part economically depressed to begin with. It now faces the additional burdens of rebuilding its demolished houses and other buildings and providing support for families whose breadwinners are dead or injured. The Pakistan Army, along with nongovernmental organizations (NGOs) and local and foreign relief workers, have been working to repair road services and restore electricity and water service. The army's delay in responding to the crisis, however, also left a hole filled by militant extremist groups, who used their knowledge of the Kashmir region to facilitate humanitarian relief and thus improve their own image and increase recruitment. Rescue efforts are hampered by the high altitude and remote location. Though progress has been made in and around Muzaffarabad, some 2,000 villages in the Kashmir region were

---

1. Development Consortium, *Social Assessment Report: Community-District Infrastructure Services Project, Azad Jammu and Kashmir* (Karachi: International Bank for Reconstruction and Development, 2001), http://www-wds.worldbank.org/servlet/WDSContentServer/WDSP/IB/2002/02/16/000094946_02020604011144/Rendered/PDF/multi0page.pdf.

not reached until weeks after the earthquake. Some areas can only be reached on foot or with donkeys.

The most difficult and urgent task is housing, with 3 million homeless in AJK and nearby parts of Pakistan. Providing shelter before the winter becomes too severe is a race against time, but there are not enough winterized tents in the world to shelter the needy. A second massive wave of deaths due to cold, hunger, and disease could come as winter sets in, doubling the casualty numbers.

Beyond the immediate relief requirements, rebuilding will take both time and money. There is also pressure to ensure that the new housing does not invite future disasters. Thus, the privately run Citizens Foundation plans construction of a model village—including 350 new homes specially designed to withstand future shocks—in Battal, in nearby Hazara district, where 500 houses were ruined. Construction was to begin in early November and is expected to take two years.[2] Local commentators have argued that this would be a good opportunity to do a similar job of modernizing the housing stock and providing better communication, health, and education infrastructure in Azad Kashmir as well.[3]

The earthquake is unlikely to introduce any fundamental change in the structure of the AJK economy—it will only add a heavy layer of reconstruction to the already difficult challenges the region faces.

Demographic and Social Features

According to the 1998 census, AJK had a population of 2.9 million. Population growth is estimated at 2.3 percent per year. The average population density in AJK is 219 persons per square kilometer. The residents are almost entirely Muslim.[4]

Most of the population—88 percent—live in rural areas and are overwhelmingly dependent on agriculture. The land is not particularly fertile. Seasonal migration to Pakistan is common, and Mirpur in particular sends a large number of young men to the Pakistan Army. Mirpur, along with Poonch and Kotli, also sends many young men abroad in search of work, either to the Persian Gulf or to the United Kingdom. Estimates run as high as 40 percent of households having a member working overseas.[5]

Nearly half (47 percent) of the urban population is located in Mirpur and Muzaffarabad. In urban areas, about 41 percent of the labor force is self-employed, 28 percent in government service and 22 percent in private employment. Some 59 percent of urban homes have a direct connection to piped water, compared to 25 percent in rural areas. Water supply through communal sources is 65 percent for rural areas, compared to 41 percent in urban areas.[6]

Literacy rates in AJK as of the 1998 census were relatively high at 61 percent (44 percent for women). This represents a substantial increase from 1981, when literacy

2. The Pakistan Newswire, "Houses Reconstruction Project Launched." Abbottabad: October 25, 2005.
3. Ershad Mahmud, "The Reconstruction Challenges in AJK," *The News* (Islamabad), October 26, 2005.
4. Development Consortium, *Social Assessment Report.*
5. Ibid.
6. Ibid.

stood at 28 percent. It is also substantially higher than the figure for Pakistan as a whole (45 percent for the whole population).[7] Local observers believe this is partly due to AJK's social structure, which is quite egalitarian compared with the quasi-feudal structures found in Punjab and other parts of Pakistan. Official AJK statistics indicate a high level of primary school enrollment: 80 percent for boys and 74 percent for girls. The enrollment figures drop sharply for higher levels of education: at the high school level, 33 percent of boys and 19 percent of girls are in school.[8] Both UNICEF and the World Bank have found the quality of primary education poor, however, due to lack of facilities and trained staff. There are few private schools, and especially after the primary level there are few schools for girls.[9]

The devastation caused by the earthquake at schools in AJK has been particularly heartrending. Work has begun on reconstructing schools. As many as 250 tents will be set up, each housing 50 children, to serve as temporary schools in Muzaffarabad and Balakot.[10] Education officers have begun clearing debris around the Balakot Higher Secondary School so that at least five classrooms can be prepared for students.[11]

Indicators of the situation of women give a very mixed picture. The sex ratio, or number of women per 100 men, is just over 100, with the districts of Mirpur and Muzaffarabad recording figures of 104 and 106 respectively. This is higher than for all of Pakistan and substantially higher than for J&K. This may reflect the high levels of male out-migration. Some local officials argue that women have tried to turn AJK's relatively strong performance in education into an advantage, though economic empowerment has been slow in coming.[12] However, the burdens of poverty, discussed below, tend to fall more heavily on women. Women are heavily represented among civilian casualties and among refugees and internally displaced persons.[13]

Income, Growth, and Poverty

Azad Jammu and Kashmir is not a prosperous area. Annual per capita income is about $184, just over 40 percent of the average Pakistan per capita income.[14] The World Bank estimates that malnutrition in the first degree affects 38 percent of the population. One survey found 35 percent of the population infected with diarrhea

---

7. Ibid.

8. Statistics Section, Planning and Development Department, Azad Government of the State of Jammu and Kashmir, "Azad Kashmir at a Glance 2002," Muzaffarabad.

9. Development Consortium, *Social Assessment Report*; see also Syed Jaffar Hussain, Tameez Ahmad, and Muhammad Mahmood, UNICEF Fact Finding Mission to Muzaffarabad-AJK, UNICEF, August 2002.

10. Associated Press of Pakistan News Agency, "Pakistan PM Says Schools in Quake-Hit Areas to Reopen Next Week," October 23, 2005.

11. Pakistan Newswire, "Meeting for Future of Valley Held," October 24, 2005.

12. Author's conversations with the secretary of local government in Muzaffarabad and with the special assistant to the AJK president in Muzaffarabad, February 2004.

13. Shaheen Akhtar, "Women and Peacebuilding in Azad Jammu and Kashmir," in *Kashmir: New Voices*, ed. W.P.S. Sidhu (Boulder, Colo.: Lynne Rienner, forthcoming).

14. "District Census Report 1998," as cited in Development Consortium, *Social Assessment Report*.

or dysentery. Only about 35 percent of the population in AJK has access to potable water.

According to the District Census Report, in AJK, the unemployment rate is between 25 and 50 percent of the economically active population. Mirpur has the lowest unemployment rate, at 25.5 percent, and Sudhnoti the highest, at 52.3 percent. These are staggeringly high figures compared to those reported in the government's Labor Force Survey for the rest of Pakistan, where the highest reported urban unemployment rates are about 14 percent, in the Northwest Frontier Province (NWFP).[15] Even making substantial allowances for flawed data and inconsistent definitions, anecdotal evidence and the available statistics suggest a desperate unemployment problem.

Official state figures show the poverty rate in AJK as one of the lowest in the country, 16 percent, compared to a high of 44 percent in NWFP.[16] On the other hand, based on local interviews and assessments of the minimum income required to support a household of 10, a World Bank assessment team concluded that the percentage in poverty would be between 30 and 40 percent, or in the same order of magnitude as Pakistan. In all districts of AJK except Mirpur, property ownership is over 90 percent. There are no ceilings on land ownership in AJK. However, most landholdings are small, with over 80 percent of farms under two hectares. The Agricultural Census of 1990 estimated that one hectare can feed a household of 10 for two months. Thus, land is widely distributed, but farms are too small to feed the families who work them. AJK's heavy dependence on remittances, however, means that the factors that increase or decrease poverty year to year include economic conditions in the countries its emigrants go to, mainly in the Persian Gulf and United Kingdom.[17]

The quality of medical care in AJK is poor, and the ratio of medical facilities and personnel to the population is inadequate. There is a pressing need for improved health care, with emphasis on malaria, pneumonia and malnutrition. In 2002, there were about 1,500 hospital beds, a ratio of approximately 2,000 people per bed. The number of people per physician was about 6,000, about four times the comparable figure for Pakistan.[18]

Besides meager agricultural and forestry earnings and government payments, the major source of income for people in AJK is remittances. The area around Mirpur has long been a recruiting ground for the Pakistan Army, and other young men, again primarily from the southern part of AJK, travel to the Persian Gulf and to Europe. One estimate indicates that 44 percent of nonfarm income, or 13.2 percent of all Azad Kashmir's income, comes from remittances.[19]

---

15. Ibid.; and Federal Bureau of Statistics, Government of Pakistan, *Labour Force Survey: 2003–2004* (Islamabad: Federal Bureau of Statistics, October 2004), http://www.statpak.gov.pk/depts/fbs/publications/lfs2003_04/lfs2003_2004.html.

16. The World Bank estimates that about 40 percent of the Pakistan population lives in poverty. Official statistics estimate that about 32.60 percent of households in Pakistan are poor.

17. Development Consortium, *Social Assessment Report*.

18. Statistics Section, Planning and Development Department, Azad Government of the State of Jammu and Kashmir, "Azad Kashmir at a Glance 2002"; World Health Organization: http://www.who.int/globalatlas.

Local Government and Institutions

AJK's development across the board, from tourism to road construction to health services, depends in large part on decisions made in Islamabad. Although nominally autonomous, AJK is financially entwined with and reliant upon the national government, which holds the purse strings. Islamabad, through the AJK council and finance secretary, lays out AJK's annual budget and sets developmental priorities.[20] There is an AJK civil service, recruited locally, but the key positions, including the finance secretary, chief secretary, and inspector general of police are "federal positions" appointed by Islamabad.

The state government is the largest nonagricultural employer in AJK, with 75,000 employees, half of them in the education system.[21] Transfer payments from the AJK government support the refugee population, which is described in greater detail below. The AJK government in turn receives a majority of its income from the federal government. It has increased its own revenue generation from 24 percent of total revenues in 1985–1990 to about 40 percent in 2000.[22] It obtains some royalties from electricity generation at Mangla Dam, located on the border with Punjab. But the high level of transfer payments on which the population depends ultimately comes from the Pakistan government.

AJK's status, as governed by Pakistan but not completely united with it, has led to some interesting initiatives on the part of the local government. Especially in the ministries charged with local government and with education, AJK residents have tried to use the region's separate status as an opportunity to innovate and to develop more effective and responsive local institutions. This may also have contributed to the relatively high level of school enrollment and literacy. There appears to be an important self-help tradition in AJK, and this has led to some mobilization of local resources and manpower to build roads, schools, and dispensaries.[23]

On the other hand, AJK residents believe they draw little economic benefit from the substantial Pakistani security presence in the region. The presence at various times of training camps for militants going to J&K increased AJK's vulnerability to firing across the Line of Control, at least until the cease-fire took effect in November 2003.

Procurement for the army is centralized in Pakistan proper, and in any case there would be little for the military to buy on the AJK economy. Apart from the young men who leave Mirpur to join the Pakistan Army, the Pakistan military employs little local labor other than the occasional porter or construction worker.

---

19. As cited in Development Consortium, *Social Assessment Report.*

20. For a fuller discussion of the relationship between AJK and the government of Pakistan, see Bushra Asif, "How Independent is Azad Jammu and Kashmir?" in *Kashmir: New Voices*, ed. W.P.S. Sidhu.

21. Author's conversation with M. Siddique Khan, secretary of local government and rural development, Muzaffarabad, March, 2004.

22. Development Consortium, *Social Assessment Report.*

23. Ibid.

Infrastructure

AJK, like J&K, has untapped hydroelectric potential. According to the AJK government, AJK has the potential to generate 5,000 MW of power. Current annual per capita power availability is 232 kWh, compared to a national 216 kWh. One of the largest hydroelectric generating plants in Pakistan, a 1,000-MW installation at the Mangla Dam, is on the border with AJK. In 1999–2000, the dam generated 3.1 billion kilowatt hours (MkWh), in addition to irrigation and some measure of flood prevention.[24] The dam's storage capacity has fallen due to sedimentation, and the Pakistan government decided in 2002 to raise the dam by 30 feet, increasing available storage space in the Mangla Lake and generating an additional 120 to 180 MW of power each year.[25] The level of royalties paid to the AJK government for the dam's benefits has been disputed between Islamabad and Muzaffarabad for years, and the AJK government takes considerable satisfaction at a recent increase in royalties for them.

The Mangla Dam expansion, whose cost is estimated at Rs. 62 billion ($1.06 billion), is the only major dam-building project currently taking place in Pakistan. Several others are on the drawing boards, and all have been bitterly controversial, accentuating regional differences within Pakistan. This one is expected to submerge an additional 15,780 acres of land and to displace 44,000 people from 8,000 homes.[26] Each family displaced by the dam building will receive a payment of Rs. 300,000 plus 110 percent of the market value of its house, and a new city and several small towns will be built for resettlement. This follows the pattern established during the building of the original dam, but memories over mishandling of the earlier compensation package are still vivid. AJK will receive rights to fish, irrigate, and draw drinking water from the dam. Supporters hope that after the project has been completed around 2007, the enlarged capacity will allow for large-scale irrigation projects that will boost agricultural production in AJK and in Pakistan.[27] Most recent major dam projects in Pakistan have been very controversial and, at best, way behind schedule.

Since the October 2005 earthquake, with electric lines down all over AJK, 140,000 members of the Hydro Electric Central Labour Union have been put to work by the Pakistan Water Power Development Authority (WAPDA), restoring electric grids in Azad Kashmir and the Northern Areas (including Muzaffarabad, Bagh, Bala Kot, and Bisham).[28] The army reported that 90 percent of the electricity

24. "Mangla Dam," Pakistan Water Gateway, http://www.waterinfo.net.pk/pdf/md.pdf.

25. Muhammad Safir Tarar, "Mangla Dam Raising Project Sedimentation Perspective," International Water Management Institute, November 10, 2003, http://www.iwmi.cgiar.org/centralasia/Files/news/ Water%20Articles.htm.

26. Akram Malik, "Shaukat Pledges: No Compromise on Kashmiris Rights," *Pakistan Times*, April 29, 2005, http://pakistantimes.net/2005/04/29/top.htm.

27. Rashid Ahmad Khan, "Increasing Storage Capacity of Mangla Dam," *The Nation*, October 21, 2002, http://www.waterinfo.net.pk/artisc.htm.

28. Pakistan Newswire, "WAPDA's Workers Busy to Restore Power in Quake Hit Areas," October 25, 2005.

and 70 percent of the water supply had been restored in Muzaffarabad.[29] Press reports indicate that electricity has also been restored in Bagh.[30]

There are 8,600 kilometers of roads in AJK. Of those, 3,000 kilometers are paved, while the majority (5,500 kilometers) are fair-weather roads.[31] This is a denser road network than for Pakistan as a whole, with 647 kilometers of roads per 1,000 square kilometers of area compared with 226 for all of Pakistan. However, railroads, a widely used and very important form of land transportation in Pakistan, do not extend into AJK or the Northern Areas. And as in J&K, the transportation network is generally oriented away from the other side of Kashmir. There is in addition no direct land transportation between AJK and the Northern Areas without going through Pakistan. So any future political or economic configuration that aims at expanding linkages among the different parts of Kashmir would require substantial expansion of the road network.

AJK's roads were hard hit by the earthquake. Three weeks after the disaster, the army announced that 42 kilometers of the road between Muzaffarabad and Chakothi (on the LOC) had been reopened, with only the remaining 15-kilometer stretch to Chakothi still closed. A landslide obstructed the Neelum Valley road (also near the LOC). Only the first 7 kilometers out of Muzaffarabad had been cleared; the remainder of the road was usable only by mules. A U.S. Chinook helicopter airlifted a bulldozer to the Neelum Valley to facilitate the ongoing road work. All roads in Bagh and Rawlakot have now been reopened to all types of traffic.[32]

There are 37,721 telephone connections in AJK and 128 telephone exchanges.[33] This works out to about 80 people for every available fixed-line telephone connection. Cellular phone service exists there, but statistics on it are not available. In Pakistan, cellular phones outnumber fixed-line subscriptions by about 2:1.[34] Telephone service was also badly disrupted by the earthquake but is starting to be restored. Press reports indicate that normal use of the telephone and the Internet have once again been made possible in parts of the affected area, particularly in and around Muzaffarabad.[35]

Major Economic Sectors

Agriculture and Forestry

Agriculture is the main source of livelihood for residents of AJK. The total area under cultivation is around 170,787 hectares or 13 percent of total area.[36] In general, farm sizes are small; 84 percent of farms are less than 2 hectares.[37] The World

---

29. Iran News Agency, "Army-Work-Pakistan," October 26, 2005.

30. Pakistan Newswire, "AJK: Transport, Telephone, Internet Functioning in Muzaffarabad," October 24, 2005.

31. Statistics Section, Planning and Development Department, Azad Government of the State of Jammu and Kashmir, "Azad Kashmir at a Glance 2002."

32. Iran News Agency, "Army-Work-Pakistan," October 26, 2005.

33. Statistics Section, Planning and Development Department, Azad Government of the State of Jammu and Kashmir, "Azad Kashmir at a Glance 2002."

34. Imran Ayub, "Cell Phone Users' Number Crosses 10 Million Mark," *Daily Times* (Lahore), October 5, 2005, http://www.dailytimes.pk./default.asp?page=story_10-5-2005_pg5_7.

35. Pakistan Newswire, "AJK: Transport, Telephone, Internet Functioning in Muzaffarabad."

Bank reports that the predominant system of land use is unsustainable. Between 1980 and 1990, annual per capita agricultural production fell from 123 to 97 kilograms. Only about 18 percent of households are engaged in full-time farming.[38] Indicative 1999 figures show annual farm family income to be about Rs. 10,190 (U.S.$176), with 59.7 percent accruing from off-farm activities. There is a shortage of hand tools and implements, as well as of draft animals, which affects agricultural production. The major crops grown are maize, wheat, and rice, with minor crops being grams, pulses, oilseeds, and vegetables.[39] Two-thirds of AJK's wheat needs are supplied from Pakistan.[40]

Decreasing productivity has led to an increase in off-farm employment for men outside AJK, and part-time farming is becoming increasingly common.[41] As a result, women have taken a greater share of the responsibility in farming.

Unlike in Indian Kashmir, fruit cultivation is not well developed in AJK. The most important fruit crops are apples, pears, walnuts, and plums.[42] Both yields and quality are low. For apples, 77 percent of all fruit trees, for example, the average yield was only 8 kilograms per tree.[43] While these figures are old and are only illustrative, they do reflect a lack of development in fruit cultivation.

Forested land under the jurisdiction of the Forest Department accounts for 43 percent of the area of AJK. Half of that is used for commercial forestry. Growing population has put increasing pressure on forestry. The net loss in forest cover is estimated to be between 6,000 and 8,000 hectares annually.[44] Until the 1980s, the AJK government's priority was exploitation of forests, and it cut down far more than could be replaced; since then, there has been more of an effort at reforestation.[45] However, stories about "bootleg" logging abound, raising concerns about the sustainability of the forests and about who benefits from them now.

Tourism

In contrast to the Northern Areas, AJK has done little to attract tourists. It does not have the kind of spectacular scenery or famous "signature sites" one finds in the Northern Areas or in J&K, but it has lovely natural areas suitable for hiking and fishing. It is close to the hill stations in Murree and Nathiagali, already very popular with Pakistanis and with expatriates resident in the region. Given greater security,

---

36. Statistics Section, Planning and Development Department, Azad Government of the State of Jammu and Kashmir, "Azad Kashmir at a Glance 2002."

37. "Agriculture Census 1990," as cited by Development Consortium, *Social Assessment Report*.

38. Muhammed Khan et al., *A Socioeconomic Study of Farming Systems in Azad Jammu and Kashmir* (Lahore: Public Economic Research Institute, 1982).

39. Statistics Section, Planning and Development Department, Azad Government of the State of Jammu and Kashmir, "Azad Kashmir at a Glance 2002," as cited in Development Consortium, *Social Assessment Report*. Value figures are not available.

40. Khan et al., *A Socioeconomic Study*.

41. Development Consortium, *Social Assessment Report*.

42. Ibid.

43. Khan et al., *A Socioeconomic Study*.

44. Statistics Section, Planning and Development Department, Azad Government of the State of Jammu and Kashmir, "Azad Kashmir at a Glance 2002."

45. Author's conversations in Muzaffarabad, March 2004.

both in Kashmir and in Pakistan, these could attract local tourists and eventually international ones as well.

At present, however, the tourism infrastructure is almost completely absent. There are few lodgings suitable for visitors. For non-Pakistanis, travel to AJK requires permission from the government of Pakistan, and though this is typically granted without difficulty, the authorities usually escort visitors to a refugee camp for a formal presentation on the Kashmir problem and the refugees. However interesting the presentation and however compelling the story, this is not an attraction for most vacationers.

Refugees

The AJK government estimates that it has some 54,000 refugees from across the Line of Control, 22,000 of them in camps run by the AJK and Pakistan governments. In addition, state government officials estimate that 19,000 people were displaced by the regular firing across the Line of Control before the cease-fire took effect in November 2003.[46] The cease-fire has effectively ended the inflow of new displaced persons from areas close to the line, but it is not clear how many of those displaced have returned home. Both groups receive financial support from the AJK government. The camps are quite rudimentary.

Anecdotal evidence indicates that the most enterprising among the refugees and displaced people have made their way into Pakistan proper, especially into nearby areas of Punjab, particularly in and around Rawalpindi and Islamabad. This involves both risk and opportunity, for the government benefits they receive depend on their continuing refugee status. On the other hand, it appears that the refugee camps have effectively gotten almost all refugee children into school and have provided for inclusion in a number of important health programs, such as vaccination.

Anecdotal evidence also suggests that many of those who came across the Line of Control, especially those who came well after independence, have intermarried with AJK and Pakistani families. Even those who arrived as Kashmiri speakers in many cases are not passing their linguistic heritage on to the next generation.

International Assistance

International donors have been active in AJK in earthquake relief and will also no doubt be involved in reconstruction work. Important support has come from the United States, including vital military airlift capability. About 20 U.S. helicopters are now operating in the region, but many more are necessary. In early November, news reports indicated that fewer than 100 helicopters were flying in the area affected by the earthquake, as compared to the 1,000 that were used in the aftermath of the 2004 South Asian tsunami, and the substantial funds required to

---

46. Source: information sheet provided by the AJK government during author's visit to Ambore refugee camp outside of Muzaffarabad, March 2004. Of the total refugees, 19,000 were registered before 1990. State government figures refer to 1.5 million refugees from the time of independence in 1947 and 50,000 refugees from the wars in 1965 and 1971, but many of these people have since either moved or died.

operate those few helicopters are in danger of running out. Besides the U.S. presence, UN agencies, international NGOs, and other bilateral donors have made an important contribution. An unusual feature of the 2005 earthquake is that India offered assistance to Pakistan; the Pakistani authorities accepted it, with some restrictions, primarily on helicopters.

Before the earthquake, Pakistan, unlike India, had encouraged aid donors to develop projects in both AJK and the Northern Areas. Bilateral donors as well as the World Bank have had a major impact through their support for the Aga Khan Rural Support Program (AKRSP), whose work is described in greater detail below, in the section on the Northern Areas. In addition, there has been a series of World Bank and UNICEF projects in AJK, and bilateral donors have been active there as well. The World Bank sponsored the Northern Resource Management Project (NRMP), between 1994 and 1999. The NRMP focused on community-driven natural resource management in AJK, with a particular focus on women. World Bank projects have focused on skills training, the most important of which are para-veterinary, vegetable production, bee keeping, poultry management, nursery raising, and other vocational skills. Under the NRMP, responsibilities such as distribution of seed and fertilizers, vaccination of livestock, and provision of tree seedlings to farmers were turned over to the private sector and NGOs. The World Bank reports that women were a particularly important component of the project, and women's development committees have provided small loans to run micro enterprises. After the World Bank project terminated, the government decided to extend the program from its own resources to cover most parts of AJK. The World Bank has also provided support for education, particularly for girls.[47]

In July 2002, the World Bank started the $20-million Community Infrastructure Service Program (CISP) in AJK. The program addresses a number of infrastructure issues, including water, sanitation, flood control, local government, law enforcement, health services, and roads.[48] These projects have provided opportunities for AJK officials to be exposed to international experience and thinking and have encouraged them to take the initiative in developing model projects in AJK.

In December 2004, the Asian Development Bank agreed to lend $57 million to further efforts to improve the infrastructure in Azad Jammu and Kashmir. The project will fund social services such as health and education, rehabilitate hospitals and schools, and finance the construction of roads and bridges along with the expansion of power and water supplies.[49]

Winners and Losers

The people who have benefited most from the current situation in AJK are those who have risen to the top on the local political scene. A Kashmir settlement that

---

47. Development Consortium, *Social Assessment Report.*

48. World Bank, "AJK Community Infrastructure and Services Project," last updated September 22, 2005, http://www.worldbank.org.pk/external/default/main?pagePK=64027221&piPK=64027220&theSitePK=293052&menuPK=293084&Projectid=P071454.

49. Asian Development Bank (ADB), "ADB to Help Improve Physical and Social Infrastructure in Azad, Jammu and Kashmir, Pakistan," news release, December 23, 2004, www.adb.org/Documents/News/2004/nr2004193.asp, accessed September 30, 2005.

resulted in AJK's full integration into Pakistan—regardless of how the rest of Kashmir was dealt with—would certainly leave them with less of a claim to local power. Entrepreneurs who have made money facilitating movements of militants are also "winners" under the current setup.

On the other hand, a more normal relationship across the Line of Control, even if it stopped short of a full settlement, would open up opportunities for entrepreneurs from both AJK and Pakistan, through expanded trade and tourism. Refugees and displaced people would also be major beneficiaries of an easing of tensions, especially if it led to a revival of the economy and the opportunity for private-sector employment.

A final group would gain from normalization of economic and social relations, and even more from a peace settlement: divided families. One cannot visit AJK without hearing a great deal about divided families. The subject comes up less frequently in India and in J&K. The answer is partly political and partly mathematical: the issue is one that tends to highlight Pakistan's view of Kashmir, and divided families are a larger percentage of the smaller population of AJK compared with J&K. But events since the opening of bus service between the two sides of Kashmir suggest that the resulting social contact has been gratifying on both sides of the line. The bus service has been interrupted by the earthquake, but it is constantly mentioned as one of the services that needs to be restored as soon as possible. When it was running, it operated only once every two weeks, and its passengers were still a tiny share of the population. Kashmiris are only beginning to think about how much more gratifying a broader array of contacts would be. This suggests that the time is ripe for the kinds of economic initiatives set forth in this report—and hopefully for moving beyond them to a genuine settlement.

The Northern Areas

The Northern Areas, covering 72,496 square kilometers, is physically spectacular, with one of the world's greatest concentrations of high mountains. Most of the population lives in steep, narrow mountain valleys, and most of the area's arable land is in these same valleys. Rainfall is sparse, less than 200 millimeters per year, and snowfall can be heavy, especially at altitudes above 4,000 meters. Landslides and earthquakes are common.[50]

Population and Urbanization

The population was 870,000 in 1998, with urban population representing only 14 percent of the total. Population growth was estimated at 2.7 percent, comparable to Pakistan's national rate of 2.6 percent. The urban population is concentrated in a handful of towns, the largest one, Gilgit, having only 56,700 people.[51]

---

50. Ahmed Hasan Dani, *History of Northern Areas of Pakistan* (Islamabad: National Institute of Historical and Cultural Research, 1989); see also Usman Ali Iftikhar, "Population, Poverty and Environment: Northern Areas Strategy for Sustainable Development," background paper, IUCN.

The population is strikingly young, half of it under 15 years old. Life expectancy at birth is 56.5 years, compared to 61 for Pakistan as a whole. Infant mortality as reported in the Northern Areas Health Project Baseline Survey was 70 per 1,000 live births, slightly under the all-Pakistan figure of 81.5.[52] This seems inconsistent with life expectancy data but may reflect recent improvements in living standards that are discussed more fully below.

Educational indicators in the Northern Areas are reportedly among the worst in the country. The literacy rate in 1998 was around 33 percent. The percentage of school-age children enrolled in school at the primary level in 2002 was estimated to be 77 percent for boys and 62 percent for girls.[53] In 1995 national achievement surveys, children and teachers in the Northern Areas scored the lowest in the nation, and it was the only region in which girls scored lower than boys, reflecting serious gender equity issues.

Income, Growth, Poverty, and Social Development

The few published data on the Northern Areas suggest that it is one of the poorest areas governed by Pakistan. Statistics on the Northern Areas are unusually hard to come by and were not regularly collected before 1991. Income per capita has been variously estimated between $164 (1998) and $241 (2001), or 40 to 58 percent of the all-Pakistan figure. The percentage of people living in poverty differed little from the all-Pakistan rate, 34 percent compared to 32 percent for Pakistan.[54] Probably the most important reason for this low income is the difficulty of eking out a living through farming in a region where arable land is scarce and of marginal quality, under the difficult conditions prevailing in high mountain valleys.

The figures cited above reflect what appears to be dramatic improvement in income and living standards in the Northern Areas during the 1990s. In 1991, the first set of economic statistics gathered on the region assessed per capita income at only 31 percent of the figure for Pakistan. The poverty rate dropped by half, at a time when Pakistan's poverty rate was climbing. Even making substantial allowances for data problems, these are remarkable achievements. They reflect a general opening up of the region, including the completion of the Karakorum Highway and the resulting increase in trade and tourism.[55]

---

51. Iftikhar, "Population, Poverty and Environment." Statistics drawn from Population Census Organization, Government of Pakistan, Population and Housing Census of Northern Areas 1998.

52. Iftikhar, "Population, Poverty and Environment," p. 16.

53. Stephen F. Rasmussen, et al., "Pakistan: Scaling Up Rural Support Programs," paper presented at "Reducing Poverty, Sustaining Growth—What Works, What Doesn't and Why," a World Bank conference, Shanghai, May 25–27, 2004, p. 10.

54. The lower income figure comes from Iftikhar, "Population, Poverty, and Environment," p. 11. (The figure given is PKR 7,500, converted at an exchange rate of PKR 46 per $1.) The higher income figure and most of the remaining data come from government of Pakistan data and farm household income and expenditure surveys cited in Rasmussen et al., "Pakistan: Scaling Up Rural Support Programs," p. 11.

55. Rasmussen et al., "Pakistan: Scaling Up Rural Support Programs"; Iftikhar, "Population, Poverty and Environment."

Another factor was the impact of a region-wide program of community development launched in 1982 by the AKRSP. This foundation is a remarkable development institution with both local roots and international support. AKRSP's interest in the Northern Areas was undoubtedly intensified by the fact that there are many Ismailis, or followers of the Aga Khan, in the area. But the program has spread throughout the Northern Areas, despite the relative inaccessibility of many of the settlements in the region. Its approach involved organizing communities, working with them to identify development opportunities, and promoting the provision of services needed to address the problems of this mountainous region. Education, health, and microcredit are key tools, and at the heart of its approach is the concept of having local communities identify their own problems and take ownership of the solutions.[56] The Aga Khan Foundation runs similar programs in India, has been working with one of the most effective education programs in Bangladesh, and has set up operations in Afghanistan. It is well funded but has also received support from the World Bank and various bilateral donors.[57] The apparent success of the AKRSP suggests that with determination, good staff, and good programs, it should be possible to have a real impact on the development picture in other parts of Kashmir as well.

Major Economic Sectors

Agriculture and Forestry

The economy of the Northern Areas is overwhelmingly based on agriculture. The area under cultivation is 125,000 acres, or about 2 percent of the total land area. Some 25,000 acres are under fruit cultivation. Wheat, barley, millet, buckwheat, and legumes are the traditional principal crops of the region, supplemented and partly replaced by maize and potatoes.[58] Apricots, grapes, and walnuts are also grown here. There is a special push to export more fruit from Hunza.

Agriculture is almost entirely subsistence based. Nearly all those working in agriculture own land.[59] There are few items for export. In fact, agricultural production is inadequate to meet domestic needs. There is an estimated shortfall of food of about 18.5 million kilograms, which is offset by the Pakistan government at subsidized rates.[60]

Rainfall is sparse and occurs primarily at high altitudes. This makes irrigation essential. Visitors to the area report that ingenious systems of small-scale irrigation have made remarkably good use of the limited supplies of surface and ground water.[61] In addition, there is a scarcity of manure as fertilizer.

---

56. See evaluation commissioned by the World Bank in Steven Rasmussen et al., "Pakistan: Scaling Up Rural Support Programs."

57. Aga Khan Foundation Web site, http://www.akdn.org/agency/akf.html, accessed September 19, 2005.

58. Karl Jettman, "Northern Areas of Pakistan: An Ethnographic Sketch," in *History of Northern Areas of Pakistan: Up to 2000 AD*, ed. Ahmed Hasan Dani (Lahore: Sang-e-Meel, 2001).

59. World Bank, *Aga Khan Rural Support Program: Third Evaluation* (Washington, D.C.: World Bank, July 1996), p. 3.

60. Dani, *History of Northern Areas of Pakistan*.

An estimated 646,000 hectares of the Northern Areas, or 9 percent, are classified as forested. Between the elevations of 750 and 3,900 meters lie four zones of forestland. Subtropical forests, including pistachio and wild olive trees, grow between 900 and 1,500 meters. Above the subtropical zone, in the temperate region ranging from 1,500 to 3,600 meters, appear varieties of cedar and fir trees. Various types of juniper, pine, birch, willow, and fir grow in the subalpine region between 3,300 and 3,800 meters. At the highest elevations, alpine scrub dots the landscape.[62] There is some commercial logging in these forests, though it is hampered by the elevation and lack of good roads. There is anecdotal evidence of illegal logging, but there are no figures available. Environmental groups are concerned about the rapid rate of deforestation. One such group, the Wildlife Conservation Society, has created the Northern Areas Conservation Program because it fears that the forested valleys could be empty within 5 to 10 years at current logging rates.[63]

Tourism

Official statistics on tourism in the Northern Areas are hard to come by, but it is estimated that half of the international tourists who visit Pakistan visit the Northern Areas. The unique geography of the region attracts many visitors. Three large mountain systems converge in the Northern Areas: the Karakoram, Himalayas, and Hindu Kush ranges. These ranges contain five peaks towering over 8,000 meters, including the world's second-tallest mountain, K-2. In 2000, international mountaineering expeditions in the Northern Areas generated just over U.S.$500,000. In addition to the mountains, 15 significant glaciers rest in the Northern Areas, most notably the enormous and contested Siachen Glacier, which stretches over 685 square kilometers. The Indus River also flows through this area, and it boasts several large lakes, Rama, Sadpara, and Kachura. Wildlife living in the region attracts naturalists, who come to see the wide variety of sheep, bear, wildcats, and birds. Pakistan is preserving some of its natural beauty by setting aside the Deosai and Khunjerab National Parks.

In addition to the physical geographic attractions, the Northern Areas also encompass many important cultural features. The ancient Silk Road that connected China with the subcontinent runs through the Northern Areas. Many archaeological sites have been unearthed in the area, some dating back as far as 500 BC. Carvings and other historical footprints can be found at Chilas, Sin Nala, Gilgit, Alam Bridge, Hunza, Skardu, Shigar Valley, Astor Valley, and Yasin.

A modern road, the Karakoram Highway, was recently built on one part of the Silk Road by the Frontier Works Organization of the Pakistani Army with Chinese assistance, and it has become an attraction in itself because of its impressive engineering. The Karakoram Highway has also opened up truck trade with adjacent

---

61. Author's correspondence with Joseph Schwartzberg, University of Minnesota, August 2005.

62. Government of Pakistan and IUCN, *Northern Areas Strategy for Sustainable Development* (Karachi: IUCN, 2003), http://www.iucn.org/places/pakistan/publications/nassd.pdf.

63. Northern Areas Conservation Program, Pakistan Projects, Wildlife Conservation Society, http://www.wcs.org/international/Asia/pakistan/pakistanprojects, accessed September 22, 2005.

parts of China, and visitors to the area report a bustling bazaar full of Chinese-made consumer goods, doubtless another attraction for local tourism.[64]

---

64. Government of Pakistan and IUCN, *Northern Areas Strategy for Sustainable Development.*

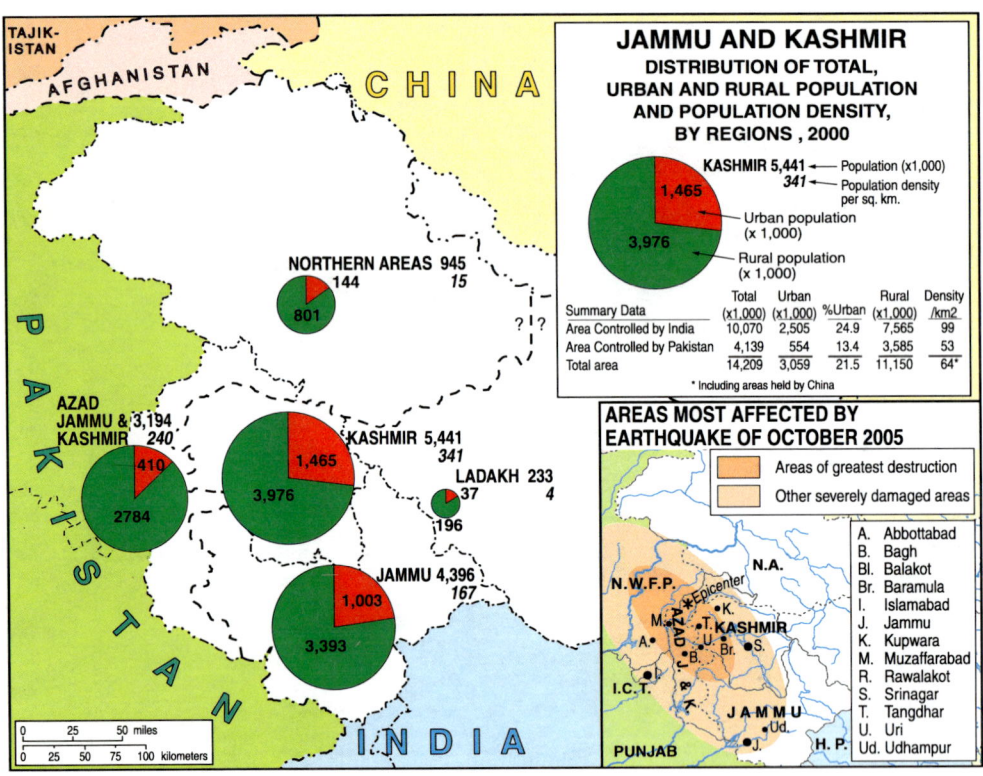

JAMMU AND KASHMIR
DISTRIBUTION OF TOTAL,
URBAN AND RURAL POPULATION
AND POPULATION DENSITY,
BY REGIONS , 2000

KASHMIR 5,441 ← Population (x1,000)
341 ← Population density per sq. km.
1,465 — Urban population (x 1,000)
3,976 — Rural population (x 1,000)

Summary Data	Total (x1,000)	Urban (x1,000)	%Urban	Rural (x1,000)	Density /km2
Area Controlled by India	10,070	2,505	24.9	7,565	99
Area Controlled by Pakistan	4,139	554	13.4	3,585	53
Total area	14,209	3,059	21.5	11,150	64*

* Including areas held by China

AREAS MOST AFFECTED BY
EARTHQUAKE OF OCTOBER 2005

Areas of greatest destruction
Other severely damaged areas

A. Abbottabad
B. Bagh
Bl. Balakot
Br. Baramula
I. Islamabad
J. Jammu
K. Kupwara
M. Muzaffarabad
R. Rawalakot
S. Srinagar
T. Tangdhar
U. Uri
Ud. Udhampur

CHAPTER 4

Recommendations

Peacemaking in Kashmir depends primarily on political decisions by the governments of India and Pakistan and leaders in Kashmir. The recommendations in this report are no substitute for this process. They could, however, help anchor a peaceful and prosperous Kashmir in a peaceful and prosperous region. They are intended to complement a political process that has started many times, most recently in January 2004, but has never been completed. In the short term, economic improvements in Kashmir can improve the economic lot of Kashmiris on both sides of the line, making them more aware of the stake they have in peace and decreasing their interest in "spoiler politics." If these economic measures are carried out with sensitivity to the security concerns of both sides, they can build confidence. In the longer term, we believe that strengthening the economic and human linkages between India and Pakistan and all parts of the old princely state of Jammu and Kashmir will make peace more sustainable and more beneficial to the people of the region.

The recommendations below are grouped topically. They start with recommendations relating to the earthquake that devastated AJK and parts of J&K on October 8, 2005, and continue with economic development measures that operate at the micro level and could produce improvements in the traditional economy, going on to include employment measures, infrastructure, tourism development, trade expansion, and measures that will connect Kashmir more fully with the world.

The October 8 earthquake created unprecedented physical destruction and loss of life. Because it was still very recent as this report went to press, our snapshot of its impact is very preliminary. But it became clear very quickly that the earthquake intensified the desire on both sides of Kashmir for greater contact and for opportunities to provide mutual support. Among the early responses was the reopening of long-closed telephone service between the two sides of Kashmir. This report includes specific recommendations for both short-term relief and longer-term disaster preparedness. But beyond that, we urge the governments in Islamabad and Delhi, and in both parts of Kashmir, to let the earthquake's destruction inspire them to reach for a bolder vision of the future and to be more ambitious in how they approach both the economics and the politics of peacemaking.

Any economic approach to Kashmir starts with improved security, which is a prerequisite for meaningful change. During a recent visit to Kashmir, the impact of security on economic activity was obvious—and negative—on both sides of the Line of Control. On the Indian side, one was constantly reminded that for most of the past decade, "life stopped at 7 p.m.," as one interlocutor put it. Even the most casual visitor to the Kashmir Valley notices the heavy presence of security personnel in the towns. Improvements in security have been fragile and short-lived. While bunkers and similar military installations are not as much in evidence as they were three years ago, police, army, and paramilitaries are everywhere.

At this writing, India and Pakistan have maintained a cease-fire since November 2003, and India is repairing the earthquake damage to a fence it had constructed along substantial portions of the Line of Control. The cease-fire led to a significant improvement in security for people living near the line, where life was able to return to nearly normal, increasing agricultural production and improving the lives of people who live nearby. The fence had helped reduce infiltration by insurgents. This more peaceful environment was also a major contribution to economic well-being, although periodic incidents involving militants, generally on the Indian side, are a reminder that this security is fragile unless a more general political understanding is reached. Most of the recommendations given below will mean little unless the cease-fire continues and the overall security situation stabilizes.

The recommendations labeled "unilateral" in this report could be carried out directly by the governments of India or Pakistan—or by the local authorities on one side or the other of the LOC. These could be implemented even without an overall political agreement and indeed could help create more favorable political conditions. We believe that the governments involved should make these improvements without waiting for the rest of the structure to fall into place. Other recommendations require private implementation.

Still other recommendations require, or would benefit by, cooperation or parallel actions by different governments, and they are labeled "joint" in the discussion below. Some of these may appear visionary under present circumstances. We recognize too that the India-Pakistan agreement with the best track record, the Indus Waters Treaty, was carefully structured to require little active cooperation. Bringing about cooperation or even parallel action by India and Pakistan is an ambitious task.

However, we are talking about building peace in Kashmir. Peace involves creating new structures and new relationships. By presenting some far-reaching recommendations here, we are trying to show how these new relationships might be crafted so as to extend the promise of an expanding global economy to the 10 million people of Kashmir, who have largely been left out. There are international precedents for economic and political changes that are just as ambitious, in countries whose quarrels have been as stubborn as the one in Kashmir. It is important to be realistic but equally important not to be imprisoned by the past.

The recommendations in this report are limited to those with substantial economic content. There are many things outside the economic realm that could and should be done to prepare the ground for a possible peaceful future for Kashmir. The fact that they are not mentioned here should not detract from their importance.

1. Disaster relief: Maximize the opportunities for a common response to the October 2005 earthquake and for coordinated preparation for future disasters.

Joint Measures

- **Move ahead in creating disaster response centers close to the LOC, with ready physical access for all communities regardless of their location.** The Indian and Pakistani governments have negotiated an arrangement for access on foot at five designated points along the LOC. This is valuable, but it should be supplemented by creating effective centers where people can go for help. Local authorities should play a major role in this effort.

- **Ensure that communities whose normal supply routes for food and other necessities have been disrupted are able to access what they need from across the LOC if necessary.** This may involve bringing in truck traffic to areas not hitherto open to trucks from the other side of the LOC. The authorities on both sides need to be creative about the security measures such an arrangement would require.

- **Examine the possibility of emergency power supplies from across the LOC, in areas where normal supplies are not available.** This could have the additional benefit of serving as a test case for an eventual grid connection, discussed later in the report.

- **Establish a joint disaster planning group,** composed primarily of local Kashmiri government officials from both sides, but also including representatives of the Indian and Pakistani governments and armed services. This group would examine the lessons learned from the earthquake and develop a plan that would work more smoothly should another disaster take place straddling the LOC. In particular, the group should develop procedures for relief access from across the LOC to communities that might be harder to reach from their own side of the line. This should be done as soon as possible, so that officials' recollections are fresh.

2. Employment: Create more opportunities for better employment.

Unemployment and underemployment are probably the most pressing economic problems on both sides of the LOC. Kashmiris consider the problem of the "educated unemployed" to be especially serious. One recent observer in J&K reports that, in the spring of 2004, three open teaching posts at a primary school attracted 2000 applicants, 900 of whom showed up to be interviewed. In AJK, the job picture is even more dismal and the tendency for talented young people to leave even stronger.

In both parts of Kashmir, and especially in AJK, the state government plays a disproportionately large role in employment, and private investment is almost non-existent. Some observers argue that for people living in J&K, only state government employment is considered a "real" job. We believe that despite this perception, what the state most urgently needs is more nongovernment jobs. This depends on investment and hence on security. The following recommendations focus on the public sector, which is likely to have the greatest impact in the short term, but a lasting solution to the employment problem depends on fundamental changes in security and in the investment climate.

Unilateral Measures

- **In both J&K and AJK, create public works jobs.** On both sides of the LOC, officials spoke about the urgent need for improved infrastructure and environmental cleanup. Projects like road building and sanitation can employ thousands and address urgent problems at the same time. Plans to bring the Indian Railways up to Srinagar offers an opportunity for substantial employment in the construction process and eventually in running the trains. Doing this effectively will also involve reining in corruption in the contracting process and cracking down on "protection rackets."

- **In AJK, link a refugee resettlement plan to public works jobs.** This is discussed in greater depth under recommendation 9, but a major obstacle to dealing with the refugee issue on the Pakistani side is the lack of jobs.

- **Expand vocational education.** Businessmen in Srinagar complain that while unemployment is high, qualified people are hard to find. They argue that "job-linked education" is badly needed. The key to success in vocational education in other places has been creating an adequate linkage to actual jobs in the marketplace. A new vocational training initiative therefore makes sense only if security has improved and it operates with the cooperation of investors willing to set up new businesses in Kashmir.

3. Economy: Strengthen the existing economy.

To create the economic conditions for peace, one must start by revitalizing the existing economy on both sides of Kashmir. The measures in this section can be undertaken unilaterally, and none of them needs to be preceded by a peace settlement. The first few measures address the rural economy, which provides the livelihood for most people on both sides of the LOC and hence deserves to have the highest priority. But we also recommend some measures that would improve the business climate in a general sense and bring in new industries.

Our recommendations for building up the traditional economic strengths on both sides of Kashmir depend heavily on the government, but they can and should try to move beyond the government as well. There are investable resources in both J&K and AJK. In J&K, annual remittances from overseas through the banking system are estimated at Rs. 45 to 50 crores (about $10 million).[1] In addition, there are significant inflows of cash from national and state government payments to individuals within Kashmir (retired state and central government servants, former militants, and many categories in between). There are also private remittances from

---

1. Author's correspondence with M.Y. Khan, chairman of the J&K Bank, June 2004.

Kashmiris resident in other parts of India. In AJK, estimates are not available, but the southern part of AJK, around Mirpur, is a prime source of emigration and hence a magnet for remittances. In both cases, much of the remittance money has been used chiefly to fund housing construction. These resources are an important potential asset for economic development.

Unilateral Measures

- **In J&K, play to traditional strengths.** Although major field crops have done badly in the past decade on the Indian side, other mainstays of the traditional economy, horticulture and crafts, have done relatively well. They have managed to capture more of the value added from their production; output has expanded. What is needed now is to build on these strengths. For example:

  - Horticulture is widely practiced and successful; invest in processing, packaging, and preservation of horticultural products. Cold storage is especially important: the lack of refrigerated storage has put J&K at a disadvantage in selling into the Indian market.

  - Expand saffron production into areas where it has not been traditionally cultivated, such as Kishtwar and Pampore.

  - Set up the kind of dairy cooperative that has been so successful elsewhere in India. Jammu and Kashmir has the largest livestock to human population in India, yet it imports these products. *Amul*, the Gujarat-based dairy cooperative, has provided a loan to set up a statewide cooperative;[2] this deserves support at the local level.

  - See also the discussion of business services under recommendation 8.

- **In AJK, invest in basic agriculture.** The economic base in AJK is particularly thin. With the exception of Bhimber and some parts of Mirpur district, AJK is not prime agricultural land. Pakistan's agricultural development efforts have largely ignored it, in part because it is remote and its population relatively small. Pakistan should look seriously at making small-scale agriculture and horticulture more diverse and more productive in AJK.

- **On both sides, create more self-sufficient community development institutions.** Both sides of Kashmir could benefit from a more active community development effort. On the Pakistani side, the Aga Khan Rural Support Foundation has a strong record in community development and micro-credit in the Northern Areas. They should be encouraged to extend their work to AJK. India boasts a wealth of excellent NGOs that are well qualified to work in this area (including the AKRSP, which has worked in other parts of India). They should be encouraged to work in J&K. The kinds of community development and micro-credit programs that would work in Kashmir are broadly similar to those

---

2. Excelsior special correspondent, "Government Announces COLA for Employees, Cabinet Discusses, Approves Budget," *Daily Excelsior* (Jammu), February 14, 2004, http://www.dailyexcelsior.com/web1/04feb14/news.htm.

in other parts of both countries. Particular needs are schools for girls and clean-water projects. On both sides, one objective of this kind of development work should be to bring new people into horticultural production, with a particular emphasis on marketing. There are good marketing-oriented programs in Sri Lanka (e.g., the Agromart program) that might be a model.

- **Explore small-scale industry in southern AJK.** Pakistan has had difficulty attracting the investment the country needs even in major commercial centers like Lahore and Karachi. But as the government tries to tackle the problems of underinvestment and of stimulating economic expansion in some of the country's most politically volatile regions, it should give a boost to the Mirpur area. Even a modest number of new investments in small-scale industry, of the sort that has been so successful in the medium-size towns in Punjab (such as sporting equipment and surgical instruments) would provide much needed job creation and would encourage the development of badly needed entrepreneurial skills.

- **In J&K, bring in more competition in the financial sector.** Industry is in a financial squeeze. In J&K, many banks closed during the insurgency, leaving the Jammu and Kashmir Bank as one of the few still operating and, for a time, as the source of more than half of all industrial financing.[3] In recent years, the State Financial Corporation has provided another source of financing. If security strengthens, it will be important to bring additional financial institutions to J&K, including micro-credit providers and institutions with experience in difficult credit environments. Another important step that could be taken is the expansion of nonbank financial centers such as post offices, which serve as a channel for remittances.

- **In J&K, AJK, and the Northern Areas, allow movie filming as security conditions permit.** The authorities on both sides have been very reluctant to allow any cinematography, whether for nature films or for commercial film production. But the number of places that really deserve to be off-limits to filmmakers on security grounds is very small. Otherwise, both types of films serve as a marvelous kind of advertising and would send the message that normality is returning. And bringing film crews in is a temporary phenomenon: a filmmaker can decide to shoot one film in Kashmir without it representing an indefinite commitment. This is an advantage in a fragile security situation.

4. Environment: Address environmental degradation.

On both sides of the line, the environment has taken a beating, and environmental protection and cleanup has been a low budget priority. But this is an essential foundation for the basic economic rebuilding that both sides need. Improving agricultural production, developing tourism, and making better use of water resources, to name only three issues discussed in this report, depend on better environmental management.

---

3. J&K DR, p. 96.

Four issues are key here: basic local environmental cleanup; water quality; forest management; and protection of the fragile Himalayan mountain ecology. The first three are discussed below; the fourth, with a proposal for an ecological park at Siachen and Baltoro glaciers, is discussed in recommendation 7.

Unilateral Measures

- **In J&K, fund urgent environmental cleanups.** Officials and business people in J&K cite environmental issues as one of their highest priorities for public investment. The specific concerns most frequently cited, including drainage, sanitation, and water quality, are vital to the region's agricultural development, urban life, and tourism. The J&K finance minister cited an estimated cost of Rs. 700 crores ($155 million) to clean up the badly polluted Dal Lake and a similar amount to address the associated drainage problems in Srinagar. These investments are critical for the quality of life of Srinagar's residents, as well as for reviving tourism (see recommendation 7).[4]

Joint Measures

- **Initiate a Kashmir-wide forest management mechanism.** On both sides of Kashmir, forests represent a major resource, one that is underutilized for economic purposes but highly vulnerable to unauthorized exploitation. Statistics are few, but anecdotal evidence abounds about illegal clearing of forests, often with the connivance of military officers and other government officials. In AJK, the state government is attempting to enforce a ban on lumbering and a reforestation drive.

  Officials from the J&K and AJK governments should develop a regular consultation process to jointly catalogue their forest resources and to develop compatible policies for managing them. A joint effort along these lines would permit forest officials to benefit from one another's expertise, but it could be carried out largely independently and would therefore be one of the easier joint projects to implement. At a later stage, it might be possible to coordinate implementation and enforcement, but that would require more extensive collaboration.

- **Create a consultative mechanism for environmental issues.** Many of the region's most basic environmental issues cross administrative and political boundaries. A joint effort to assess and deal with Kashmir's environmental sustainability should be worked into India-Pakistan talks on Kashmir's economic future at an early stage. Water quality should be high on the agenda for any such group. Since these are issues that affect people on both sides of the Line of Control, they ought to be a promising area for early India-Pakistan cooperation, setting the stage for more controversial issues like trade. One example, dealt with in greater depth under recommendation 7, is protecting the high-altitude ecosystem of the Siachen and Baltoro Glacier region.

---

4. Author's conversations with Muzaffar Baig, J&K finance minister, March 2004.

5. Transportation and communications: Improve the infrastructure.

Unilateral Measures

■ **Give priority to extending rail service to Srinagar.** Indian Railways is in the process of implementing an expansion of the rail system beyond Jammu. Its plans call for rail service to Srinagar by 2007, with service to Udhampur opening up some time before then. This project has been talked about for years; implementing it should be a high priority. It will significantly improve the marketability of Kashmiri goods in India and will make land transportation between Kashmir and the Indian plains much more reliable during the winter.

■ **Create major road repair programs in both J&K and AJK.** Even before the earthquake, the roads on both sides of the LOC were inadequate to carry a volume of trade that would afford Kashmiris a decent life. Officials in both regions cite road improvements as a high priority. After the earthquake, the urgency is even greater. Improving the roads need not wait for an improvement in the political situation and can generate employment as well.

■ **Modernize communications in J&K.** At present, land-line phone service in J&K is unreliable, and the only cell phones that work are from a service that is restricted to J&K. The reason for this is the security services' concern that making normal cell phones available will benefit militants. However, once they took the step of allowing some cellular service, there remained little logic to the restrictions. The poor service affects the modern economy across the board and effectively rules out investment in J&K by India's booming information technology industry. The government needs to integrate Kashmir into the India-wide cellular phone setup and put energy and funds into expanding telephone service around the state.

The same goes for expanding Internet access and other electronic communications. J&K's hotels and industries need to be plugged into the world through modern electronics. Economically, isolation is deadly in today's world. Politically, this same isolation undermines peace efforts and accentuates the alienation that has made the Kashmir problem so difficult to deal with.

■ **Expand internal civilian air links inside J&K.** Once security has improved to the point where a significant increase in tourism takes place, there will be a market for internal air services. Srinagar, Jammu, and Leh are linked by air. There are other "outstation" destinations that could much more easily be reached by air, if security conditions permit. Improving airports in the major towns in the valley and other areas that have the potential for attracting significant numbers of tourists could increase tourism in Kashmir and, more importantly, spread the benefits of the tourist economy to a wider section of Kashmiri towns.

Joint Measures

- **Open the Srinagar-Muzaffarabad road to trucks and trade; open additional road links such as the one between Poonch and Rawalakot.** In April 2005, a biweekly bus service was inaugurated between Srinagar and Muzaffarabad. It started under very difficult circumstances: militants had bombed a tourist facility where the passengers intending to travel from the Indian to the Pakistani side were spending the night. Since then, however, the buses rolled without incident until the October 2005 earthquake destroyed the road. The determination of both the Pakistani and the Indian government to carry on with the long-heralded bus service, and the Kashmiris' interest in traveling, seem to have deterred further violent action, and the bus route has been the scene of some of the earliest post-earthquake repairs.

  After over a year of negotiations, India and Pakistan reached a compromise agreement on documentation for travelers on the bus service. Each country supplies the buses that travel on its side of the Line of Control, and the passengers must carry entry permits, rather than passports and visas.[5] There have been fitful efforts to limit bus travelers to Kashmir, but this stricture has not been enforced; a group of political figures from J&K visited AJK and went on to Islamabad.

  The idea of bus travel was popular from the start, especially in the Kashmir Valley. Part of its appeal is psychological: it is seen as a breach in the isolation from which Kashmir has suffered for the past half century. After the earthquake, the service was popular enough to inspire calls on both sides for an early restoration of service. A bus every two weeks, however, does not provide opportunities for travel to very many people, and if the process stops there, it is likely to revive the cynicism that is never very far from the surface in Kashmir.

  Hence the importance of building on this successful experience by opening up additional channels for travel and by allowing trade between the parts of Kashmir. In April 2005, when President Musharraf visited Delhi, he and Prime Minister Singh announced that they would move toward more frequent bus service, an additional bus route between Poonch and Rawalakot, and authorization for truck traffic and trade on the original Srinagar-Muzaffarabad road. Subsequent high-level meetings between Indian and Pakistani officials have reaffirmed these decisions, and they have also figured in meetings between the Indian prime minister and separatist leaders from J&K.

  These announced road openings should take place as soon as possible, and others should follow. Opening up trade will have tremendous psychological

---

5. The documentation issue sounds arcane, but it is an example of the kind of practice that can derail important political initiatives. The decision reached for travelers on the intra-Kashmir bus also sidestepped another little-discussed documentation issue. The government of Pakistan normally annotates the passports of residents of AJK as "citizens of the state of Jammu and Kashmir," and the government of India had the practice of refusing visas to Pakistanis with such markings on their passports.

significance and will add to the participants' stake in peace. The potential for trade, and the other measures needed to encourage it, are discussed below (see recommendation 8). Just as importantly, as Indians, Pakistanis, and Kashmiris all see the two governments following through on promises they have made, it becomes easier to imagine reaching and keeping agreements on the more difficult aspects of India-Pakistan relations and on Kashmir.

- **Restore rail links between India and Pakistan through Kashmir.** The confidence-building measures that India and Pakistan have undertaken to work on include the restoration of rail links between Munabao and Khokrapar, in Rajasthan and Sindh respectively, by January 2006. Once that is done, the two governments should work on restoring the old rail link between Jammu and Sialkot, as well as the one linking Srinagar with Muzaffarabad, Abbotabad, and Rawalpindi. Both the capacity of railways for carrying increasing numbers of people and increasing amounts of goods, and the symbolism of restoring the physical infrastructure of travel, will restore a much needed sense that connecting Kashmir to the surrounding region is normal and durable.

6. Water and energy: Take advantage of the state's resources.

Both sides of Kashmir have substantial hydropower potential, and both want to develop it. Earlier sections of this report discussed the Indus Waters Treaty of 1960 and its impact on the development of Kashmir, through which flow the three western rivers in the Indus system, whose waters the treaty assigned to Pakistan.

AJK is a major producer of electric power, and much of this power supplies the rest of Pakistan. The government of Pakistan has recently begun to award royalty payments to the AJK government from the Mangla Dam, on the border between AJK and Pakistan. A new dam on the Pakistan-AJK side of the Neelam River, now under construction, will substantially expand the power supply to Muzaffarabad and will connect to the Pakistani national grid.

On the Indian side, the energy potential is there, but the Indus Waters Treaty imposes restrictions on the type of water storage structures that can be built. Two major dams have been built within these restrictions, but others have proved controversial. Small run-of-the-river plants are often worth building but require a decentralized approach to investment, generation, and distribution. India has initiated three major water and power projects, which Pakistan has challenged under the treaty.

In considering how water and power development could be used to benefit Kashmir and develop peace constituencies there, we do not recommend redrawing the basic division of water between India and Pakistan as defined in the Indus Waters Treaty. That instrument has been an effective means of resolving water disputes for over 40 years and should not be put at risk until the relationship between India and Pakistan has undergone substantial transformation. Our recommendations focus instead on joint efforts to make new hydropower supplies available to both countries and to Kashmiris on both sides of the line.

Joint Measures

- **Resolve outstanding Indus Waters Treaty issues.** The two countries disagree on several projects in J&K. The Wullar barrage/Tulbul navigation channel is a long-standing item on the list of issues India and Pakistan discuss. India's work on a dam at Baglihar is currently the subject of an adjudication process involving international experts under the treaty. India has also begun work on a new dam on the Kishenganga (Neelam) River. In all three cases, differing interpretations of the Indus Waters Treaty have been the occasion for disputes that are really caught up in the larger tapestry of India-Pakistan relations. In the case of Baglihar, Pakistan is also concerned about the possibility of downstream flooding. And Pakistan's general shortage of water gives heightened importance to all three issues. Settling them would provide economic benefits in Kashmir, as well as signal a large step forward in India-Pakistan relations.

- **Connect the electricity grids that service both sides of Kashmir.** The strongest economic linkage between the two sides of Kashmir, and ultimately between India and Pakistan, would come from connecting the two electricity grids. India has talked with Pakistan about buying electricity during periods when Pakistan has a surplus, but they have never reached agreement. Besides the two countries' difficult political relationship, the fact that electricity prices in Pakistan are significantly higher than those in India has been an obstacle. But a grid connection would also increase both the stability and the amount of power available to both countries. It could also provide the context for developing hydropower resources that are now out of reach because of Pakistani concerns about the Indus Waters Treaty, water availability, and other factors. These benefits should give officials an incentive to negotiate a creative solution to the price problem.

  At the moment, both the Kashmir issue and the problem of political risk from strategic trade between India and Pakistan stand in the way of work on grid connection. But a serious study of how the job could be done technically, and how the political risk could be managed, would be a tremendous contribution to the "tool kit" of peacemakers in both countries.

- **Develop procedures for joint investment in electric power to benefit both sides of Kashmir.** Both the Indian and Pakistani public-sector power authorities are in financial crisis. In both cases, the problems involve weak collection of fees, corruption, reluctance to allow privatization to move too far ahead, and government fiscal problems. Consequently, the funds for developing the power sector are woefully short of projected demand. In both countries, the authorities have recognized for some time that this will require private-sector investment in the power sector, but in both countries the first efforts along those lines have been fraught with financial and political problems.

  It seems quixotic, against this background, to suggest joint India-Pakistan foreign investment in electric power in one of the most insecure parts of the subcontinent. Recognizing that this idea may not come to fruition for a long time, we nonetheless recommend developing a blueprint for how it might take place. The amount of money involved could be as much as $10 billion over 10 years.[6] Such a program would require not only expert economic and engineering work, but as importantly, careful planning so that these new developments could fit within the framework of the Indus Water Treaty. A joint process involving the two national governments, Kashmiri experts, and an institution with international convening power like the World Bank would be the best way to approach this complex issue.

■ **Create a joint group charged with assessing and improving water quality.** A group of Indian, Pakistani, and Kashmiri scientists could look at the question of water quality and water usage in Kashmir. Two issues in particular come to mind. First, they could work together to monitor the quality of water flowing through Kashmir, assessing contamination levels and suggesting remedies. The work initiated in 2003 by the Cooperative Monitoring Center of the Sandia National Laboratories in Albuquerque, New Mexico, on joint monitoring of water flow and quality regulation in the Indus River system might provide a useful precedent.[7]

Second, this group could examine patterns of farming and water use on both sides of Kashmir that would conserve both the quantity and the quality of water used in agriculture. Given the looming shortages of water throughout the Indus system, this would be a real contribution not only to Kashmir's future but to the whole region.

7. Tourism: Rebuild the industry.

J&K is well known as a tourist destination, famous for its wonderful scenery, beautiful mountain meadows, hiking and trekking, houseboats, the striking mountains and monasteries of Ladakh, and several important Hindu and Buddhist pilgrimage sites. At its high point, in the late 1980s, the tourism industry accounted for an estimated 15 percent of the gross domestic product of J&K, and when one considers the people indirectly dependent on tourism, the percentage was even higher. While people speak of a tourism boom since early 2003, the number of tourists is only about one-third of the figure for the late 1980s. Even more than other industries, tourism depends critically on the reestablishment of security, particularly in the major tourist towns of J&K and along the roads. The J&K government has provided "refurbishment credits" to those who operate tourism facilities (hotels, transportation companies, etc.), but these still require the owner to take a considerable risk, since he needs to put up and begin repaying the money for refurbishment up front, without being sure whether sufficient business will develop.

On the Pakistani side, tourism is undeveloped. AJK has relatively few "signature sites" that would be a logical nucleus for tourist itineraries, but it does have lovely scenery and magnificent hiking and fishing. The Northern Areas, on the other

---

6. Shahid Javed Burki, "Kashmir: The Economic Option," *DAWN* (Karachi), July 19, 2005.

7. See Gaurav Rajen et al., *South Asia Transboundary Water Quality Monitoring Workshop: Summary Report* (Albuquerque, N.M.: Cooperative Monitoring Center, Sandia National Laboratories, April 2003), www.cmc.sandia.gov/links/cmc-papers/sand2003-0696.pdf. The Cooperative Monitoring Center promotes regional partnerships among scientists and researchers—in this case, in South Asia—focusing on common security objectives.

hand, have attracted a small but steady stream of tourists, including mountaineers and visitors, both local and foreign, who want to drive up into the mountains along the Karakorum Highway. Modest facilities have grown up beside the highway. Much of the scenery in the Northern Areas is spectacular and several locales, most notably Hunza and its surroundings, have become quite popular, especially among young and hardy travelers.

India and Pakistan, as well as the J&K and AJK authorities, can and should help the tourism operators rebuild through normal investment support programs. But the most powerful support for peace building from the tourism industry would come from joint interventions.

Unilateral Measures

- **Develop new tourist sites in J&K.** Most of the focus until now has been on the area immediately around Srinagar and Dal Lake. If security improves in the rural areas and small towns, it should be possible to develop the tourist potential of other lakes in the valley. This would involve creating new accommodations and improving the accessibility of other lakes through better roads and better arrangements for hiring cars with drivers. Adding air services to this mix—helicopter or executive jet—would require more ambitious improvements in security.

- **Build up facilities for hiking and fishing in J&K, AJK, and the Northern Areas.** Nature has provided magnificent places to explore; still needed are expanded accommodations, trained guides, and markings for trails that can be used for these purposes. Mountaineering organizations are already active; we recommend extending this kind of activity to hiking and trekking organizations.

Joint Measures

- **Develop an ecological science park incorporating parts of the Siachen and Baltoro Glaciers.** At present, this area is the world's most desolate and forbidding military confrontation point. Even before the current cease-fire, more soldiers died of cold, pulmonary edema, accidents, and other noncombat causes than of wounds sustained in battle. And their sacrifices contributed little to either country's security. India and Pakistan nearly a decade ago came close to reaching agreement to disengage their forces from Siachen, but ultimately the agreement fell apart. Following the Kargil conflict of 1999, in which Pakistan's operations on the Indian side of the Line of Control aimed at cutting off India's access to Siachen, the Indian government and army has become more reluctant to change the status of Siachen. Both sides privately recognize, however, that the Siachen outposts have little strategic military significance. Demilitarization of Siachen is once again under active discussion between the two countries.

Once the area is demilitarized, a science park, created with the consent and cooperation of both sides, could be a powerful symbol of the peaceful new relationship India and Pakistan would like to create. The primary goal of the park would be to promote ecosystem conservation of a rare high-altitude mountain range and to provide opportunities for responsible mountaineering, recreational tourism, and research. The scientific value of the park has been spelled out in a paper issued by the Sandia National Laboratories.[8]

At least two different groups have floated proposals along these lines. The most comprehensive description was elaborated at a meeting hosted by Professor Saleem Ali at the University of Vermont in October 2003. It proposes establishing a conservation and memorial park in the Karakoram Mountains adjoining existing conservation parks and reserves. It might start within the area covered by the Central Karakoram National Park, with a possible eastward and southward extension in future years. Management of the park would be cooperative, involving both governments, as well as local communities, and would be carried out in accordance with established criteria for cultural landscape management under the International Union for the Conservation of Nature. It would be important to have direct access from both the Indian and the Pakistani sides. The precise plans for such a park would need to be developed by Indians and Pakistanis. Some preliminary suggestions are included in a separate paper prepared by the group that met with Professor Ali.

A similar proposal was put together by two visiting scholars at the Sandia National Laboratories, Brigadier General Gurmeet Kanwal (Indian Army) and Brigadier General Asad Hakeem (Pakistani Army), in the context of a paper describing how demilitarization of the Siachen area might be carried out. They proposed that a science center be run by an international civilian team including international and regional scientists.[9]

- **Establish a joint Kashmir Tourism Development Board, with primarily private membership.** Tourism is one of the sectors in which the development of AJK and J&K can be complementary. A joint tourism development board would be a concrete manifestation of the "soft borders" that can help anchor a peaceful Kashmir in a peaceful region.

  This board would be composed chiefly of representatives of the private tourism industry (such as representatives of the hotel, transportation, and crafts industries). It should include representatives of the state and local governments from J&K, AJK, and the Northern Areas. It would facilitate the development of facilities and commercial packages that permit tourists to visit different parts of Kashmir on the same trip. Representatives of the Indian and Pakistani governments could participate and would be especially helpful in ensuring that the two countries' visa requirements and transportation networks do not undercut the objective of fostering joint tourism.

---

8. See Kent L. Biringer, *Siachen Science Center: A Concept for Cooperation at the Top of the World* (Albuquerque, N.M.: Cooperative Monitoring Center, Sandia National Laboratories, May 1995), http://www.cmc.sandia.gov/links/cmc-papers/sand-98-0505-2/index.html.

9. Presented at a meeting at the Henry L. Stimson Center, Washington, D.C., September 8, 2005.

8. Encourage trade and investment linkages outside the state.

Three types of out-of-state trade are important to Kashmir's economic future: domestic trade, or trade between J&K and the whole of India, and between AJK and the whole of Pakistan; cross-line trade, between communities close to both sides of the Line of Control; and international trade. All three can be expanded now, with good effects on the economic well-being of Kashmiris. A more ambitious approach to all three ought to be considered an essential ingredient in a settlement.

Domestic Trade—Unilateral Measures

- **Build up transport infrastructure and local industry, especially in J&K.** The measures recommended above (see recommendations 2 and 4) will give a particular boost to all-India trade. Of particular importance is the creation of refrigerated shipment capability, both by land and by air. This would open up all-India markets to such perishable Kashmiri products as strawberries and cherries.

  In addition, especially in the Jammu area where transportation links to the rest of India are stronger and short-term security problems fewer, small-scale industrial development has considerable potential.

Cross-Line Trade—Joint Measures

- **Create points on the Line of Control where nearby communities can trade.** There are communities in Kashmir, such as the Gujjars, whose traditional economic livelihoods span the Line of Control. Others, such as Kupwara, Poonch, the Neelam Valley, and most of AJK, have a disproportionate number of divided families. After more than 50 years of separation, these communities have had to adapt and create new economic arrangements. But there is almost certainly a market for buying and selling basic food and consumer items within a few kilometers of the Line of Control. And the recent earthquake has underlined the importance of these kinds of links.

  This is the classic "border trade" situation. In other cases, the Indian and Pakistani governments have been willing to allow such trade; the recent agreement between India and China allowing border trade between Sikkim and adjacent parts of China comes to mind. This would supplement the proposed initiation of truck trade along the Muzaffarabad-Srinagar road, which President Musharraf and Prime Minister Singh have said they intend to permit. Establishing designated points where local trade could take place would be a logical first step. It could build on the agreement already reached for five border crossing points for people needing help with earthquake relief. The Indian government has floated the idea of "meeting points" along the Line of Control. This recommendation expands that idea to allowing trade. It would be as valuable for its political symbolism as for the economic opportunity it provides.

- **Study the potential market for J&K horticultural products in Pakistan.** Fruit growers in J&K have high hopes that the opening of direct truck traffic between

Srinagar and Muzaffarabad will provide them with a substantial new market on the plains of Pakistani Punjab. Once the road is fully open, the area around Rawalpindi and Islamabad will be a shorter and easier drive from the Kashmir Valley than the Indian plains. This is worth a serious economic assessment, to take into account the potential supply from the Kashmir Valley, relative prices, standards, and other possible obstacles to trade. If the potential is significant, India and Pakistan should agree to give priority to horticultural products as well as Pakistani goods with a potential market in Kashmir in their negotiations on bilateral trade.

International Trade—Unilateral Measures

■ **In J&K, establish the business services needed to support expanded exports.** Kashmiri producers are currently not able to export their goods directly from Srinagar, but must work through brokers in Delhi. Just as Kashmiri producers of horticulture and crafts saw their domestic trade increase when they took over the distribution function, direct exports would provide a significant boost to Kashmiri producers, especially to small businesses. We recommend providing "one-stop shopping" for at least the following key services:

  • A "dry port," where exporters could take care of all their packaging, documentation, and customs processing requirements

  • Bonded trucking and rail service

  • A container depot—availability of *small* containers would be essential, as the road tunnels between Kashmir and the Indian plains will not accommodate 40-foot containers

The state government had established a "one-stop shopping" facility in the past. It was sold to the state-owned Indian Airlines and then closed down early in the insurgency.[10] Since that time, both air transport and transportation infrastructure have been opened to the private sector. Indian-owned private airlines already service Srinagar and Jammu. The operation of several airports elsewhere in India is being privatized, but the airport in Srinagar is owned by the military and is also an air force base. But changes in the way transportation and related services are provided in India should make it easier to establish a modern export-processing facility based on a public-private partnership.

In addition, to facilitate inbound trade, the state government should establish streamlined procedures and facilities for checking trucks on entry into the state.

■ **Designate Srinagar Airport an international airport for both goods and passengers.** As indicated in the earlier part of this report, the government of India is working on an expansion of Srinagar Airport and on designating it as an international airport by the time the 2006 tourist season starts. This would be a boost to the tourism industry. It would open up new markets, permitting pack-

10. Author's discussions with members of the Srinagar Chamber of Commerce, February 2004.

age tours combined with other destinations in India or in the region. Allowing direct international access to Srinagar Airport will also increase the effectiveness of our recommendations on combined J&K/AJK tourism. A significant first step would be to allow direct charter flights from Europe and Asia, as these are potentially large sources of tourism revenue.

But the airport also needs to handle international cargo. Taken together with the business services recommended above, this would make the export distribution chain for Kashmiri products shorter and less expensive, providing a further export boost.

Investment—Unilateral Measures

Central government economic revival packages have typically included tax incentives designed to spur investment in J&K. They have had little effect, principally because the main deterrents to investment are too fundamental to be affected by incentives that operate at the margin.

The most important obstacle to investment in J&K, as we have noted several times, is insecurity. There are others, notably the poor reputation of government institutions and of law enforcement in the state. The recent Transparency International survey that found J&K second only to Bihar in corruption is only the most recent illustration of a problem that has been widely discussed for decades. A serious effort to bring into the state the investment needed to truly revive the economy will need to be accompanied by a real push for greater transparency and accountability in state economic institutions.

Observers of Pakistan have made similar comments for years. The recent increases in private investment in Pakistan suggest that it is possible to start this kind of reform process, though much remains to be done. The investment climate in AJK and the Northern Areas suffers from the same disadvantages as Pakistan's, and the relative remoteness of both regions adds an extra challenge.

Besides the tax and other investment incentives that both sides have used, and the by now standard observation that improving security is the essential first step to boost investment, we recommend the following:

- **Focus on encouraging small-scale investment first.** As a practical matter, investment for the next several years will be overwhelmingly Kashmiri and will come in relatively small individual projects. This means that small-scale investments and financing facilities for relatively small operators will have more effect than those oriented toward major national or international-scale enterprises.

9. Internal refugees: Begin addressing the problems.

On both sides of Kashmir, refugee or displaced populations have become a highly potent symbol of national frustrations with the Kashmir issue. Everyone who talks about a stable Kashmir solution envisages refugee populations returning to their original homes, but little or nothing is being done to create either the political or the economic underpinnings for a solution to the refugee problems. These are within the control of each side acting alone but are politically difficult to tackle.

■ **In J&K, include the requirements for the return of the Hindu population—the "Pandits"— to the Valley of Kashmir in any dialogue among the central government, the state government, and Kashmiri separatists.** The Pandits who left the Valley of Kashmir, most of whom are now living either in Jammu or near Delhi, feel neglected by all levels of the political system. They remain committed to returning to the valley, as a group rather than in small numbers. They appear to have virtually no dialogue with the Muslims of the valley, though this would be the most important prerequisite for the kind of reconciliation they want. Dialogue between the central government in Delhi and the Kashmiris, especially the separatists, has tended to lag during periods of India-Pakistan dialogue. As those political contacts resume, the refugee issue needs to be on the agenda because bringing these people back to the valley will require careful preparation and uncharacteristically deft political handling by both the Kashmiris and the Indian government.

■ **In AJK, create a refugee employment and resettlement program.** There is no plan for resettling the 54,000 refugees in AJK, and giving up one's refugee status involves loss of valuable government funding. Although refugees are free to take jobs outside the camps, there are few jobs available. This is an inherently unhealthy situation. The government of Pakistan is understandably reluctant to take any action that makes it look as if it accepts the current division of Kashmir, and it already has between 1.2 and 1.8 million Afghan refugees in other parts of the country. But refugee resettlement, coupled with a serious jobs program, would be a tremendous investment in an eventual peace. A plan that in principle allowed for future resettlement on either side of the LOC, while providing a link to newly created jobs in AJK, would be a good place to start.

10. Connect Kashmir with the world.

Beyond these specific economic measures, it is important to connect Kashmir with the world outside of India and Pakistan. Educational and cultural ties can help to broaden Kashmiris' focus beyond their immediate political situation and can change the perception of Kashmir in the outside world.

Unilateral Measures

■ **Give greater international reach to Kashmir's cultures, especially the one associated with the Kashmiri language, "Kashmiriyet."** Kashmir has been largely defined, in international perceptions, by the dispute over its status, and Kashmiris as people and as a culture have become almost invisible. With private and local government support, musical performances, poetry readings, and other demonstrations of Kashmir's rich and diverse cultural heritage could give Kashmiris a new voice and presence as people on the international circuit. The most powerful means of providing this voice would be through privately funded activities that would avoid being drawn into using Kashmiri culture as a political statement. Programs at U.S. universities that already have strong South Asia programs offering courses on Kashmiri culture, language, and history would also be useful.

Joint Measures

- **Expand people-to-people opportunities.** There has been significant growth in travel between India and Pakistan since January 2004, and travelers have been received on both sides with real enthusiasm. The Srinagar-Muzaffarabad bus, and more liberal Indian policies permitting Pakistanis to visit Kashmir and Kashmiri separatists to visit Pakistan, have begun to make Kashmiris participants in this process. This needs to continue and expand, and it should extend to travel to other parts of India and Pakistan.

- **Create an exchange program for business students.** Many types of student exchange would be valuable, but business studies are particularly promising because both India and Pakistan boast world-class business schools—the Indian Institutes of Management (IIMs) and the Lahore University of Management Sciences (LUMS), respectively. A modest scholarship program could make it possible for students from the Kashmir Valley to study at LUMS, and for students from AJK to study at one of the IIMs. Such a program would be most effective if it were undertaken and funded as a joint effort between Indian and Pakistani businesses interested in joint ventures focused on Kashmir.

- **Create exchange programs for university faculty.** The universities in Kashmir—Jammu and Srinagar Universities on the Indian side, AJK University on the Pakistani side—could start by developing a few common courses, in which two universities could conduct video-conferenced classes, with professors at both ends collaborating. This would be most interesting if the courses dealt with problems common to both parts of Kashmir, such as the environmental impact of diminishing forest cover, or irrigation management, or perhaps Kashmiri language and literature. Eventually, this could broaden into a series of visiting exchange professorships.

This arrangement could usefully be broadened to universities elsewhere in India and Pakistan. There is a well-developed network of Indian and Pakistani professors who have ongoing professional relationships at events outside the region and who would be the logical nucleus for such an effort.

11. Long-term vision: Kashmir as a model for an integrated region.

Our final recommendation is more visionary and more ambitious than the rest: to develop both sides of Kashmir as a special economic zone, with free trade access to India and Pakistan and with the authority to accept investment from both countries and from abroad. In its most comprehensive version, this arrangement could serve as a model for the kind of dynamic trade and investment policies that both India and Pakistan are trying to put in place on a national scale. The idea would be to anchor a more prosperous and secure Kashmir into a more integrated and peaceful region.

Even an idea as ambitious as this one does not necessarily need to wait for a settlement. The outline sketched out below consists of steps that could be taken cooperatively by the governments in Islamabad and New Delhi and by the state and local authorities in J&K, AJK, and the Northern Areas. The national authorities could agree to treat the relevant parts of Kashmir as a special zone for purposes of trade and investment policy. In consultation with the local authorities, they would make parallel changes in the parts of the state for which they had responsibility and would continue expanding economic contacts among the different parts of Kashmir. As with the bus service that was inaugurated in April 2005, they would pragmatically acknowledge the Line of Control, without attempting to define or change the line's international status.

Background and Context

Trade among the member countries of the South Asian Association for Regional Cooperation (SAARC) is surprisingly small, chiefly on account of these countries' relatively recent move to liberalize trade. Some 80 percent of the total consists of trade between India and each of the six other members. Only Nepal and Bhutan, both of them highly dependent on economic relations with India, conduct more than 15 percent of their overall trade within the region.

The SAARC decision in 2004 to move toward a regional free trade area by 2006 was an effort to force the pace of both political relations and trade liberalization in the region. Progress has been slow, as one might have expected given the high trade barriers in the region and governments' skepticism about who will benefit from more open trade. The experience of the India–Sri Lanka free trade agreement signed in 1999, however, suggests that even where trade is very lopsided in India's favor, both parties to a trade agreement can benefit significantly.

Trade between India and Pakistan is even more heavily restricted than the South Asian norm. Pakistan maintains a specific list of items that are permitted in trade with India. Though India formally extends normal, or most-favored-nation (MFN) treatment to imports from Pakistan, the level of actual imports is so small that it is hard to avoid the conclusion that there are other informal restrictions at work. Two-way trade is currently 1 to 2 percent of the two countries' total trade. The business communities in both India and Pakistan have generally been in favor of liberalizing trade. The principal barriers have been political. India has, for years, urged Pakistan to grant MFN treatment, whereas Pakistan has preferred to move slowly on bilateral trade liberalization until substantial progress has been made on Kashmir. Movement toward open trade within SAARC puts India-Pakistan trade liberalization into a political context that is much easier for the government of Pakistan to deal with.

Kashmir is essentially left out of what little trade there is, except to the extent that modest local trade may develop once the Indian and Pakistani governments open up a truck route between the two sides of Kashmir.

There is a precedent in both India and Pakistan for establishing areas where special economic policies apply. Export promotion zones (EPZs) are already an established policy tool in both India and Pakistan. In India, these zones require legislation at both the state and central level. They offer the developer of the zone a variety of income, service, and state-level tax exemptions, freedom from pricing restrictions, exemption from licensing requirements for power generation and distribution, and duty-free materials. Investors setting up operations in the zone enjoy a package of tax exemptions, certain exemptions from licensing, foreign exchange and other regulatory requirements, flexibility in labor laws, and authorization to accept foreign direct investment without caps on foreign ownership, including in areas normally reserved for small-scale industry.[11] These zones account for about 4 percent of India's exports, and the value added represents about half the value exported.[12] The incentives available in Pakistan are broadly similar.[13]

A special economic zone of the sort we are proposing would differ from the existing zones in important aspects: it would be much larger, would include large areas of traditional agriculture, and would involve parallel regulation in parts of the state with different national authorities in charge. But the idea that there can be areas with different economic rules is already in operation.

- *Key elements.* Designing a special economic zone proposal should be the subject of a much longer and more detailed study. The special economic zone could include all of J&K, AJK, and the Northern Areas, or it could be restricted to a more limited area. But since the concept would be intended to create a region that enjoys free trade and joint investment with both Pakistan and India, it would need to cover substantial territory on both sides of the Line of Control, including at least the Valley of Kashmir and AJK. We have attempted to outline here a few of the key provisions, in particular those governing investment, trade, and infrastructure.

- *Investment.* The investment rules India and Pakistan apply to EPZs would be a good starting point for a special economic zone in Kashmir. It would be essential to preserve, and perhaps improve, the regulatory streamlining that normally goes with an EPZ and to build into it speeded-up approval for joint investments involving Indians and Pakistanis—especially involving Kashmiris from both sides. Regulatory simplification is more important than tax breaks.

- *Trade.* The typical trade rules for EPZs focus on facilities needed to produce goods for export: availability of duty-free plant, equipment, and inputs, and drastic simplification of the processing of both imports and exports. Adapting this concept to the Kashmir situation, the most important thing would be to ensure that goods produced in whichever parts of the state were included in the special economic zone and could be shipped to India or Pakistan duty free. A streamlined procedure for documenting exports would be key, whether these were duty-free exports to India or Pakistan or regular exports overseas. It would be desirable to give the Kashmir zone the same duty-free access to plant, equipment, and inputs that is available to EPZs. The United States and other outside

11. Presentations to World Bank–sponsored conference, New Delhi, April 2004, by D.K. Mittal, former joint secretary, Ministry of Commerce, Government of India, and Arun Narula, executive director, Mahindra and Mahindra.

12. See Brijesh Pazhayathodi, review of *Free Trade Zones (FTZs) to Special Economic Zones (SEZs): The Great Indian Dream*, by Thothathri Raman and Parag Diwan, *Reserve Bank of India Occasional Papers*, vol. 24, nos. 1 and 2 (Summer and Monsoon 2003), http://www.rbi.org.in/scripts/publicationsview.aspx?id=5912.

13. Presentation to World Bank-sponsored conference, Karachi, March 2004, Prvaiz A. Sankhla, general manager (investment promotion), Export Processing Zones Authority, Government of Pakistan.

trading partners could provide an additional incentive for investing in a Kashmir special economic zone by granting duty-free access to goods containing inputs from both sides of the Line of Control. A similar arrangement was put in place in 1998 to encourage cross-investment between Jordan and Israel, and an agreement to that effect was signed in December 2004 by Egypt, Israel, and the United States.[14]

■ *The infrastructure issue.* One of the attractions of EPZs for investors is good infrastructure. At present, infrastructure, especially power and telecommunications, is weak on both sides of Kashmir. To attract investments to a special economic zone, reliable power and telecommunications services that work throughout Kashmir and throughout India and Pakistan would be a requirement.

Creating substantial areas with reliable power supply would require a major investment, which would almost certainly have to be carried out in close cooperation with the local and perhaps national governments. For telecommunications, the restrictions on connectivity currently in force would have to be lifted by government, but once this is done, private telecommunications operators could do the rest of the job. A joint infrastructure development board with private and public participation might be a vehicle for agreeing on priorities in making these improvements. This is an area where international assistance, from bilateral or multilateral donors, could be helpful.

■ *Making it work.* To make an idea like this work, it would be important to persuade a few businesses to act as pioneers for joint investments. Ideally, some of the largest Indian and Pakistani businesses could start, together with Kashmiri enterprises. This might attract foreign partnerships and, eventually, smaller businesses from the rest of India and Pakistan.

The *tourism* sector would be an excellent candidate for this type of investment. It has the advantage of a major private-sector role, so that it would not involve meshing the operations of two different public-sector units with their somewhat more rigid operating styles. *Transportation* would be another candidate. There is already at least one Indian company interested in investing in Pakistan for training in *information technology*; this kind of investment could take place on either side of Kashmir. As discussed elsewhere in this report, *electric power* would be a particularly valuable area for joint investment, although it would be more complicated in light of the large role of the government in power generation in both India and Pakistan.[15]

A special economic zone would place new demands on governance on both sides of Kashmir. It would require joint efforts to prevent the smuggling of

---

14. Emad Mekay, "Egypt Signs on to U.S.-Israel Model," IPSNEWS, December 15, 2004.

15. For a similar proposal, see Shahid Javed Burki, "Kashmir: A Problem in Search of a Solution," unpublished paper prepared for the U.S. Institute of Peace, Washington, D.C., October 31, 2004.

arms, drugs, currency, and other forms of contraband. It would require regular consultations between local authorities.

- *Impact.* A special economic zone in Kashmir would be the most powerful possible symbol of the new relationship India and Pakistan are trying to build and of their commitment to free trade within SAARC. The short-term impact on the trade statistics might be modest, since the main exports from both sides of Kashmir are products that neither country imports on any significant scale. But given peace and a transformed India-Pakistan relationship, investment would have a chance to pick up, and new export markets would follow.

Foreign Financing and Next Steps

A number of the measures recommended here could benefit from donor financing. Pakistan historically has welcomed donor involvement in AJK. The World Bank approved a Community Infrastructure and Services Project for AJK in 2002.

On the Indian side, the Asian Development Bank approved a $250-million development project in December 2004 to rehabilitate water services in Jammu and Srinagar and rebuild roads and bridges in 14 districts around the state. This is the first multilaterally funded development project since 1983.[16] Bilateral donors, however, are not allowed to operate in J&K. As the government of India develops new initiatives in Kashmir, we hope it will decide to encourage bilateral assistance to J&K. The involvement of both bilateral and multilateral aid agencies, together with improved security, could boost investment and consequently make a dent in the region's severe unemployment problem.

In addition, there are many NGOs within India, as well as private business organizations and state and central government authorities, that would be able to undertake the kinds of measures we suggest.

Putting an estimated value on economic rebuilding and integration in Kashmir is an almost impossible task. However, when one considers that the potential for expanded India-Pakistan trade is estimated at up to 14 percent of the two countries' current total; that more efficient use of energy, especially for power generation and transportation, is one of the biggest foreseeable drains on both countries' economic future; and that the tradition of horticulture and handicrafts in J&K has nurtured entrepreneurship throughout the population, the potential for improving the lives of Kashmiris is enormous.

---

16. Asian Development Bank, "Report and Recommendation to the Board of Directors on a Proposed Loan to India for the Multisector Project for Infrastructure Rehabilitation in Jammu and Kashmir." Previous multilateral projects, all from the World Bank, were J&K Horticulture, 1978; Social Forestry (including J&K), 1983; and Himalayan Waters, 1983.

About the Author

Teresita C. Schaffer came to CSIS in August 1998 after a 30-year career in the U.S. Foreign Service. She devoted most of her career to South Asia, on which she was one of the State Department's principal experts, and to international economic issues. From 1989 to 1992, she served as deputy assistant secretary of state for South Asia, at that time the senior South Asia position in the department; from 1992 to 1995, Schaffer was the U.S. ambassador to Sri Lanka; and she served as director of the Foreign Service Institute from 1995 to 1997. Her earlier posts included Tel Aviv, Islamabad, New Delhi, and Dhaka, as well as a tour as director of the Office of International Trade in the State Department. She spent a year as a consultant on business issues relating to South Asia after retiring from the Foreign Service. Her publications include "Kashmir: Fifty Years of Running in Place," in *Grasping the Nettle* (USIP, 2004), "Sri Lanka: Lessons from the 1995 Negotiations," in *Creating Peace in Sri Lanka* (Brookings, 1998), two studies on women in Bangladesh, CSIS reports *Pakistan's Future; Rising India and U.S. Policy Options in Asia;* and several reports on the HIV/AIDS epidemic in India, as well as articles in several scholarly and popular publications. She has taught in the past at Georgetown University and American University. Schaffer speaks French, Swedish, German, Italian, Hebrew, Hindi, Urdu, and has studied Bangla and Sinhala.

About the Kashmir Study Group

The Kashmir Study Group, founded in 1996, is a private association including academics and foreign policy specialists with lengthy professional experience with South Asian issues and prominent U.S. legislators. Members of the group hold differing views on the Kashmir problem but are united in the conviction that the conflict must be resolved in a manner that is peaceful, honorable, and practical for all concerned. In an effort to contribute to such a solution, the group has published several innovative approaches to the Kashmir issue.